THIRD EDITION

handbook of
PHYSICAL THERAPY

Robert Shestack, Ph.G.R.P., P.T.R.

*Director, Department of Physical Therapy, Washington County
Hospital, Hagerstown, Md. Director and Consulting Physical
Therapist at the Fahrney Keedy Memorial Home for the Aged,
Boonsboro, Md.; the Kemp Horn Training Center, Smithsburg,
Md.; and the Mount Lena School for the Mentally Retarded,
Smithsburg, Md.*

SPRINGER PUBLISHING COMPANY
New York

To my dear wife Mary (Miriam), the mother of our beloved daughter Debby. "The house is the Temple of the woman, the education of her children her Divine Service, and the family her Congregation" (Talmud).

Copyright © 1977 by Springer Publishing Company, Inc.

First edition 1956
Second edition 1967
Third edition 1977

Springer Publishing Company, Inc.
200 Park Avenue South
New York, N.Y. 10003

79 80 81 / 10 9 8 7 6 5 4 3

Library of Congress Catalog Card Number: 66-30317

Standard Book Numbers: 0-8261-0173-9 (cloth edition)
0-8261-0174-7 (paper edition)

Printed in the United States of America

CONTENTS

PREFACE TO THE THIRD EDITION

The purpose of this third edition of the *Handbook of Physical Therapy* is to summarize, in concise, reference form, the most common indications for physical therapy and the modalities in current use. It is intended for the professional and paraprofessional health worker in the general hospital. We make no claim to completeness, but the information given should enable health workers to approach the field of physical therapy with greater assurance and discrimination when planning for the management of their patients.

Treatments involving elaborate therapeutic exercise and other complicated technics have been avoided because total rehabilitation programs require the cooperation of a team of medical and technical specialists and a vast array of special equipment. Since the average stay of a patient in a general hospital is from seven to ten days, the facilities required for extensive rehabilitation as currently practiced are not usually found in the physical therapy departments of these hospitals. Patients in need of such treatment should, if feasible, be referred to rehabilitation centers that are staffed and equipped to meet their particular needs.

Early application of physical therapy is often an important factor in shortening the period of convalescence and hastening complete recovery. Even patients still confined to bed can receive appropriate forms of physical therapy with advantage and safety. Exercise designed to improve the circulation in the extremities and to minimize pulmonary congestion will help to counteract general debility, loss of appetite, thrombophlebitis, embolism, and other complications frequently encountered in persons who must undergo prolonged bed rest. Other early treatments tend to minimize muscular atrophy, loss of range of motion, and/or contractures.

In this edition we have stressed only the generally accepted methods of treatment that have been successfully used by many critical practitioners. The selection of a particular method is the responsibility of the referring physician and depends upon his judgment of each patient's needs.

ACKNOWLEDGMENTS

I would like to thank the publishers, organizations, pharmaceutical companies, and several individuals who gave permission to reproduce various charts and tables in this book. In addition to those cited in the text, I am grateful to the Riker Laboratories for permission to use material from their booklet *Living with Asthma, Chronic Bronchitis, and Emphysema* (1966) in my discussion of these conditions. Special thanks are due to Mrs. Helen D. Behnke for her excellent editorial advice and cooperation in the preparation of the manuscript for this book.

FOREWORD TO THE FIRST EDITION

The role of physical medicine in the therapeutic armamentarium has witnessed a marked upsurge in recent years. The need for restoration of many casualties in the late wars, the invention of new modalities that make use of technological advances, and the easy availability of therapy machines have all served to stimulate the use of physical therapy. The training of the doctor in the value of these methods, their contraindications, and even in their practical applications has not kept pace with this development. All too often the doctor is limited in his knowledge of the various types of treatment that can be used, the specific capabilities of each of them, and the methods of getting the most out of them. The erudition of articles on waves and frequencies and the limited approach of manufacturers' brochures are helpful but leave a substantial gap in the fund of knowledge necessary for the practical use of physical therapy. It is therefore quite proper that a book be made available that presents the subject concisely from the point of view of the practicing therapist.

In this volume the subject matter is covered in a practical manner by a man who is engaged in the actual use of physical therapy. It is presented in his own way and is based on his personal experience. His many years of work in this field qualify him for this. The information that he can give should prove valuable not alone to the physical therapist but also the physician who in the course of his practice makes use of physical therapy.

I. William Nachlas, M.D.
Associate Professor of Orthopedic Surgery,
Johns Hopkins University, School of Medicine

I

GENERAL
CONSIDERATIONS

1
PHYSICAL THERAPY — AN OVERVIEW

Physical therapy, or physical medicine, as it is now known, is the newest and yet the oldest field of medical practice. It is the newest because only in the past fifteen to twenty years has it come to be recognized as an integral part of regular medicine. It is the oldest because physical agents have been used in the treatment of disease for thousands of years. The primitive man who crawled into the sunshine to receive the benefits of its warmth and vitalizing effect started the practice of heliotherapy; the first man who bathed a wound in some stream instituted the practice of hydrotherapy; and the first man who rubbed a contused or bruised muscle introduced massage.

Ancient physicians knew about and employed physical agents in therapy. They even employed electrotherapy in the form of shocks from electrified torpedo fish in the treatment of certain diseases. The Romans practiced hydrotherapy and thermotherapy in the Roman baths. The Greek gymnasts used massage and corrective exercise.

The modern revival of the use of physical therapy modalities began during World War I and was greatly accelerated during and after World War II. All branches of government and private agencies now allocate millions of dollars each year for rehabilitation, through physical therapy, of injured, diseased, or handicapped children, adults, and aged persons. This form of treatment is particularly helpful to patients with orthopedic, neuropsychiatric, arthritic, and pre- and postoperative chest conditions; to those who suffer from cerebral palsy or peripheral nerve or spinal cord injuries; to those who have had strokes, amputations, industrial or automobile accidents; and to hemiplegics and paraplegics.

Physical medicine may be defined as the treatment of patients' disabilities from disease, injury, or loss of a body part with therapeutic exercise, heat, cold, water, light, electricity, ultrasound, or massage. It is a branch of medical science and is

3

conducted under medical supervision; that is, before treatment, every patient is examined by a physician who diagnoses the patient's condition and prescribes the physical therapy treatment.

The objectives of physical therapy depend, of course, on the condition being treated, although many factors enter into decisions as to type of therapy to be employed. In general, all objectives are stated in terms of increasing or restoring the ability of the patient's body, or any of its parts, to perform normal functional activities. Specifically, physical therapy objectives include:

1. Increasing and maintaining strength and endurance
2. Increasing range of motion in joints
3. Increasing coordination
4. Decreasing pain
5. Decreasing muscle spasm and spasticity
6. Decreasing swelling
7. Decreasing chest congestion
8. Promoting the healing of soft tissue lesions
9. Preventing contractures and deformities
10. Decreasing abnormal sensory feedback
11. Correcting postural deviations
12. Decreasing gait deviations
13. Promoting independence in ambulation
14. Promoting independence in elevation activities
15. Promoting independence in transfer activities
16. Teaching patients and/or their families how to correctly carry out physical therapy procedures in the patient's home

THE PHYSICAL THERAPIST

Since physical therapy is a specialty within the field of medicine, it follows that those who become therapists must meet certain educational requirements.

Forty-four college or university programs in physical therapy, which admit both men and women, are approved by the American Physical Therapy Association and the Council on Education of the American Medical Association. Graduation from high school is a prerequisite for admission to these programs, which provide from four to six years of instruction and lead to baccalaureate and masters degrees. The curriculums for these programs include courses in applied science, anatomy, physiology, neuroanatomy, kinesiology, pathology, psychology, physics, neurology, orthopedics, pediatrics, surgery, electrotherapy, hydrotherapy, massage, radiation therapy, therapeutic exercise, physical rehabilitation, and physical therapy as applied to medicine.

Physical therapists work in general, military, public health, and crippled children's hospitals, in physicians' offices, public and private clinics and outpatient departments, mental institutions, sanitariums, schools, industrial and manufacturing plants, health resorts, and college and Y.M.C.A. athletic departments. Between 80 and 90% of 7,000 selected hospitals in the United States have physical therapy departments. There are between 18,000 and 20,000 registered physical therapists in the country, although the need is estimated at 25,000 and the projected need for 1980 is 30,000 to 35,000. Physical therapists are required to be licensed. Certain treatments may be given by aides or assistants, but always under the close supervision of a licensed therapist.

THE PATIENTS

Approximately 265,000 American men were permanently disabled as a result of combat injuries sustained during World War II, 40,000 persons annually undergo amputations, nearly 200,000 American children are afflicted with cerebral palsy, and thousands of persons are crippled yearly as a result of automobile or industrial accidents. Their rehabilitation, through physical therapy, consitutes both a responsibility and a challenge to workers in the field of physical medicine.

2
ORDERING PHYSICAL THERAPY

The physician who requests physical therapy for a patient needs to know what types of physical therapy equipment and what modalities the hospital department has at its disposal, and whether physical therapy has been found to be beneficial in other patients with similar conditions. He also needs to talk to the therapist about the patient's condition and about the particular treatment he orders.

The following basic principles will guide the physician who prescribes physical therapy:

1. Therapy should be begun as soon as possible in the course of treatment.
2. Conditions of long standing usually require treatment over a considerable time; one or two treatments will not produce the desired result.
3. Intervals between treatments should be relatively short; some treatments are given daily, others two or three times a week. For most conditions, treatments given only once a week are worthless.
4. Cost should not prevent the patient from receiving treatment, for two reasons: a) when indicated, physical therapy will often effect a saving because it will enable the patient to return to his regular occupation sooner; and b) the cost of treatments is covered in most health insurance plans.
5. All prescriptions for treatment should be ordered in writing. This is necessary for accuracy and advisable for legal reasons.
6. Prescriptions should not call for the simultaneous use of more modalities than necessary. For example, an order should not call for heat, massage, and exercise when exercise alone, or heat and massage without

exercise, would be sufficient to produce the desired effects.

7. The patient who is receiving physical therapy should be seen by his physician at least every two weeks, or oftener if necessary to evaluate the effects of the treatment.

8. If the use of a certain modality does not result in improvement, this does not necessarily mean that physical therapy is contraindicated, but it might mean that the physician will change the prescription to a different modality.

THE PRESCRIPTION

The selection of appropriate physical therapy procedures requires a knowledge of the physiological effects, dosage, frequency, and usual duration of the treatments, and of how they may be adapted to the specific needs, general condition, and peculiarities of the individual patient. With these facts in mind, the prescription should state clearly the patient's primary and secondary diagnoses, the results desired, and the specific treatment ordered, and it should be modified as the patient's condition changes.

Suggested forms for ordering physical therapy treatments and for recording treatments given may be found in Appendix I at the end of this book. Specifically, every prescription for physical therapy should be dated and should contain the following information:

1. The patient's full name, address, and telephone number
2. The patient's age
3. The patient's diagnosis
4. The specific area to be treated
5. Instructions to the therapist — dosage, frequency of treatment, and how long the treatment is to be continued
6. The specific modality, or modalities, to be used
7. Special information needed by the therapist (whether

the patient has a cardiac condition, has certain anesthetic areas, is diabetic, etc.)

8. The date the patient is to return to the physician for a checkup, if this is known
9. The signature of the physician who orders the treatment

II

MODALITIES USED
IN PHYSICAL THERAPY

3
HEAT AND LIGHT

Heat is one of the most commonly prescribed modalities in physical therapy. The physiologic effects of heat are analgesic, antispasmodic, decongestive, and sedative. Heat increases the exchange of oxygen and hastens absorption of exudates. It is a vasodilator that increases the amount of blood brought to a region; it also increases metabolism locally. When vasodilation, relief of pain, or muscular relaxation is desired, heat may be prescribed as a therapeutic agent. It is often used before massage and exercises are given.

The therapist must keep in mind, however, that there are certain contraindications for the use of heat. Heat should not be applied to anesthetic areas or areas in which there is loss of the perception of heat and cold. Patients who should not receive heat therapy also include those with high fever, decompensated heart disease or peripheral vascular disease, and those with a metallic or thermoplastic implant in an underlying area. The presence of a malignant tumor (except in the terminal stage) is another contraindication to heat therapy.

MOIST HOT PACK

The moist hot pack is the most commonly used means of applying heat; it is widely used in physicians' offices, physical therapy departments, and patients' homes. The heating unit for moist hot packs consists of a small, stainless steel water tank equipped with a thermostatic control that maintains packs at a constant temperature of 170°F. The manufactured pack, consisting of a fabric envelope containing silica gel which absorbs and holds a great deal of water, has been found useful in hospitals, offices, and patients' homes. After it is immersed in the tank of hot water, it becomes a hot compress that provides 30 minutes of intense moist heat. The degree of heat applied may be controlled by increasing or decreasing layers of

11

towelling between the skin and the hot wet pack. Moist heat therapy can be used two or three times a day. There is certainly less danger of burning the patient with these packs than with hot water bottles or heating pads as they are commonly used by lay persons.

Indications for Use

The moist hot pack is effective in relieving muscle spasm associated with acute lumbosacral sprains and low back pain. Bed rest with frequent applications of the pack will gradually restore the muscles in spasm to normal condition, after which light massage may be used.

Such packs are also useful in acute tendonitis or acute bursitis since they help overcome spasm in the muscles of the involved shoulder girdle. (During the acute stages of these conditions, better results will be achieved from the application of ice packs.)

The moist hot pack is also very effective in treatment of a painful knee. In these cases the muscle spasm must be alleviated before therapy involving the use of such modalities as massage and/or exercise is employed.

Because of their flexibility and ease of placement, moist hot packs can be used to treat several affected areas simultaneously. For the patient with generalized arthritis that involves multiple joints, the advantage of being able to treat a number of joint segments at the same time is obvious.

Other conditions in which moist hot packs have a beneficial effect include:

Abscess, acute	Myositis
Carbuncle	Neuritis
Cellulitis	Sprains, 24 to 48 hours
Cystitis	after injury
Epicondylitis	Strains, 24 to 48 hours
Fibrositis	after injury
Fractures, after bivalving	Synovitis
or removing cast	Tenosynovitis
Hemorrhoids	Torticollis
Myalgias, all forms	Wounds

Contraindications

Anesthesia of the area to be treated

The presence of cardiovascular disease, decompensated

The presence of a malignant tumor (except in the terminal stages)

Peripheral vascular disease (intense local application is contraindicated)

Sensory disturbances that lead to loss of perception of heat and cold

Certain arthritic conditions that are aggravated by heat (acute stages, or when the skin is inflamed)

INFRARED RADIATION

Radiant heat is heat that is transmitted through the air from the infrared portion of the spectrum. Infrared radiation for physical therapy is produced primarily by various types of heat lamps and bakers, but radiant heat may also be provided by objects such as household electric heaters, stoves, hot-water bottles, electric heating pads, and heated bricks.

Heat lamps and bakers, however, have many advantages over hot-water bottles and heating pads. They require little of the therapist's time and attention and provide constant heat for any desired length of time without any variation in the degree of heat being applied and without danger of burning the patient. They do not come into contact with the body part being treated, and thus there is no weight or pressure on the part; therefore, it is possible for the patient to remain undisturbed for prolonged periods of time. The heat produced by bakers and lamps is more effective than that produced by other sources of radiant heat and the therapeutic effects are more predictable.

Infrared rays are heat units. The infrared coil used in therapeutic lamps does not differ from the coil used in the household electric heater. The difference is in the reflectors; household heaters have a wider reflector which diffuses the heat throughout the room, whereas the therapist's infrared lamp has a more concave reflector which converges the radiant heat on a small area. The household heater, used at close range, may be a fair substitute for a therapeutic heat lamp, although the flatter reflector will tend to disperse the heat.

Infrared Generators

Luminous Type

This type of generator consists of tungsten or carbon filaments heated to high incandescence, either in a glass bulb mounted at the focus of a concave reflecting mirror or in a conical bulb (of clear or red glass) with the reflecting mirror built into the inside of the funnel-shaped part. About 30% of the total radiation emitted is of wavelengths that can penetrate from 1 to 10 millimeters into the skin. Luminous sources of radiation furnish more penetrating heating and are therefore preferable for treatment of traumatic conditions affecting deeper parts. The bulbs come in various wattages, from a few to 1,500 watts. The shape and size of the reflector is important. If the reflector is not constructed for use with a specific lamp, hot spots, shadows of the filament, or irregular patterns of heating will result. The lamp, together with the reflector in which it is housed, is held in position by stands of various shapes and heights, so arranged that they may be held in the hand or clamped on chairs or tables. Floorstands are the most convenient, because they allow the lamp to be correctly placed to focus on the injured area of the body.

For application of luminous heat to the extremities, the old tunnel-like "baker," consisting of a polished reflector on supporting legs, is still the most serviceable. Four to sixteen 60-watt carbon or tungsten filament bulbs are attached to the underside of the reflector. These luminous heaters are employed very effectively in chronic stages of rheumatoid arthritis. Baking, properly and systematically performed and coupled with massage, may work wonders in the treatment of painful stiff shoulders, knees, and other joints.

Nonluminous Type

This type of generator consists of heating elements of resistant materials placed in a suitable reflector. The heating unit may be made of coils of resistant metal wire wound around cylindrical or cone-shaped pieces of porcelain or other such material. Other units are made of circular plates or disks of resistant metal or rods of Carborundum. When this type of generator is placed in a suitable reflector it eliminates hot spots, has no filament shadows, and distributes the rays evenly over the treatment area. These infrared generators are equipped with reflectors placed on stands that can be moved easily. Lamps come in sizes from 75 to 1,500 watt input. This type of nonluminous infrared generator is easy to operate, has no glare, and can be used for a long time.

Patients sometimes favor one heat source over another. Some are bothered by a bright light, whereas the full glow of infrared makes them feel comfortable. This occurs especially when the face is being heated and also with restless children. In acute, painful conditions, radiation from a nonluminous source has a more soothing effect.

Physiological Effects

Infrared radiation penetrates only superficially, usually to a depth of less than 10 millimeters. It increases blood flow in the normal circulatory tree, relaxes muscle spasm when there is no central nervous system pathology, and relieves pain in the subacute and chronic stages of various forms of arthritis and neuritis, and in orthopedic disabilities when there is no tendency to edema. Infrared rays cause sensations of warmth or burning on the surface of the body. These sensations are felt instantly and erythema is produced almost immediately. This thermal erythema, which is often mottled, disappears rapidly after cessation of exposure.

Usually, any source of infrared radiation is used once or twice daily for 20 or 25 minutes, with the source being about 18 inches away from the area to be treated. When applying infrared heat to the face, the eyes should be protected by pieces of absorbent cotton moistened with water and flattened against the eyelids. The exposed skin is generally covered with a towel before the lamp is turned on.

Indications for Use

Abscesses
Arthritis — subacute and chronic, selected forms
Bell's palsy
Bronchitis
Carbuncle
Cellulitis
Contusions, 24 to 48 hours after injury
Dislocations, after reduction
Epicondylitis
Fibrositis
Fractures, after cast is removed
Furuncles
Gout
Low back pain
Lymphangitis
Mastoiditis
Muscle and tendon injury
Myalgia
Osteomyelitis
Phlebitis, subacute
Pleurisy, dry and nontubercular
Pleurodynia
Rhinitis
Sinusitis
Sprains, 24 to 48 hours after injury
Synovitis
Tenosynovitis
Thrombophlebitis
Wounds or incisions in which hyperemia is desirable (e.g., after surgical repair)

Contraindications

Diminished or abnormal thermal sensory thresholds
Cardiovascular disease, decompensated
Hyperpyrexia
The presence of an implant (metallic or thermoplastic) in the underlying area
The presence of a malignant tumor (except in terminal stages)
Peripheral vascular disease

Special Precautions

1. The tolerance of the skin to heat is different in various parts of the body and in different individuals.
2. When applying heat, cover the exposed area with a towel. Do not apply heat directly to the skin.
3. A large lamp or baker is more effective than other heat sources for all but small areas.
4. Small lamps should be used at a distance of 16 to 18 inches and bakers at a distance at which they produce a comfortable warmth.
5. Electric bulbs or hot metal should not come into contact with the skin.
6. A 30-minute treatment two or three times a day is more effective than one long period of continuous heat.
7. Baking an arm, leg, or back should be continued for 30 to 45 minutes, at least, to obtain any therapeutic benefit.
8. Massage should follow the heat treatment unless contraindicated.
9. The part treated should not be cooled or chilled immediately after heat has been applied.
10. A 15- to 30-minute rest period following baking and massage is beneficial.

DIATHERMY

Diathermy is a technique of elevating the heat of body tissues by passing a shortwave high-frequency current through part of the body. The heat results from resistance offered by the tissue to passage of the electrical current.

Physiological Effects

All so-called high-frequency currents penetrate more deeply than infrared radiation. Hence, the patient receiving diathermy should never have as great a sensation of heat as when exposed to infrared energy. The physiologic effects are the same as those produced by infrared radiation except that there is better volume heating of the tissues with high-frequency currents. Depending on the frequency and type of electrode used, penetration of the current varies from 1 to 3 centimeters.

Dosage, Duration, and Frequency of Treatment

The regulation of dosage in shortwave diathermy is empirical. It depends on the comfortable heat sensation of the patient's skin. In high-frequency machines, the milliammeter indicates not the electrical energy passing through the patient but the amount passing through the machine. Therefore, the patient's tolerance is the most important guide to be used for determining the dosage.

Medical diathermy should be a pleasant procedure at all times and never cause pain during treatment or damage to the tissues. The initial strength of the current should be adjusted in accordance with previous experience and be guided by the patient's sensation. The generally accepted method of grading dosage at present is to keep within the feeling of comfortable skin warmth, according to the acuteness and location of the pathological condition. In painful sensory conditions such as neuritis and neuralgia, or acute inflammatory conditions of the skin and inner organs, one may start the treatment at an energy output sufficient to cause a feeling of comfortable warmth, then decrease the output to just below that sensation, so that the patient has practically no sensation of heat. In deep chronic inflammations, the energy output may be just below the grade at which a burning sensation occurs.

Since the patient's sensation of heat is the principal guide for regulation of dosage, it is imperative that his sensory perception be normal or near normal.

In acute conditions and early in the course of treatments when the degree of reaction is uncertain, a small amount of energy should be applied for about 15 minutes. Occurrence or aggravation of pain indicates that the current is too strong or has been applied for too long a time. The average duration should be between 25 and 30 minutes, never more. Excessively long treatments may cause an intensive heat effect and thereby exhaust the patient.

Start with a few treatments every day, then continue every other day. Acute and very painful conditions or recent injuries, in which the early return of function is essential, require daily treatment. With improvement of such conditions this frequency can be reduced. For the average patient with a chronic ailment, treatment on alternate days usually suffices and may be administered less often, as the patient's condition improves.

Indications for Use

Chronic arthritis

Contusions

Muscle strain

Respiratory conditions accompanied by soreness in the chest, pain, coughing, viscous secretions, sinusitis

Musculoskeletal conditions accompanied by pain, muscle spasm, or infection

Neurological conditions, especially sciatica

Contraindications

Certain acute inflammatory processes

Acute nondraining cellulitis

Acute infectious arthritis

Conditions in which there is a tendency to hemorrhage, e.g., gastric ulcer

Peripheral nerve injuries over areas in which the sensation of heat has been lost

Pregnancy, if treatment of the abdomen, pelvis, or lower part of the back is required

Menstruation

When a malignant growth is suspected in the area to be treated

Special Precautions

Before applying shortwave diathermy, metallic objects, hairpins, safety pins, buttons, keys, knives, watches, and buckles should be removed from the field of treatment because they lead to a concentration of electrical energy and the possibility of burns. Metallic chairs or tables, radiators, water pipes, electrical fixtures, or other grounded metal should not be within possible contact with the patient. Conducting cables should not make contact with such objects. Treatment tables and chairs should not have any metallic parts. Cables leading to the apparatus must not cut across each other or get too close to each other, as this may lead to overheating of the insulation and fire. Shortwave diathermy should be applied to the unclothed body only. A burn received from a treatment by shortwave diathermy, when the clothes have not been removed, might readily provoke a medicolegal situation. After treatment it is important to inspect the skin of the part treated.

ULTRAVIOLET RADIATION

Ultraviolet therapy utilizes the ultraviolet portion of the light spectrum, that is, the portion that lies beyond the visible spectrum. Ultraviolet rays are of high frequency and short length. For physical therapy, ultraviolet radiation is provided by a special lamp. The therapist, or anyone else using such a lamp, should know the difference between "sun" lamps and "therapeutic" lamps. The chief difference is that the spectral radiation characteristics of sun lamps are such that they are suitable for home use by persons familiar with the action of natural sunlight, and without the supervision of a physician. Therapeutic lamps, however, have spectral emission characteristics that necessitate professional supervision or control to avoid hazards of overexposure.

A sun lamp, to comply with the requirements for minimum intensity, should generate sufficient ultraviolet energy to produce a minimally perceptible erythema on the average untanned skin in not more than 60 minutes, at an operating distance of 24 inches.

If the intensity is such that a minimally perceptible erythema may be obtained in 15 minutes at a distance of 24 inches from reflector to patient, the unit is classified as a therapeutic lamp.

Physiological Effects

Ultraviolet rays have an actinic (or chemical) action. They produce latent erythema (in contrast to infrared rays, which produce immediate erythema) which appears several hours after exposure. Following intensive irradiation of the skin with ultraviolet rays, the latent erythema is, in turn, followed by changes in the pigmentation of the skin.

Ultraviolet radiation results in increases in the metabolism of calcium, phosphorous, and protein, and thus is useful in attenuating or reversing early or moderate cachexia. It is also useful as an adjunct in the treatment of certain emotional disturbances. The bactericidal, bacteriostatic, and fungicidal effects of the rays are helpful in the treatment of a variety of pathological conditions.

Dosage

Dosages of ultraviolet radiation should be prescribed according to the reaction desired rather than duration of exposure. There is wide variation in individual response to ultraviolet therapy, erythema of the skin being the most evident. It readily indicates an individual's sensitivity to ultraviolet, and for this reason is taken as the criterion for establishing dosage. Men are more sensitive than women; blondes more so than brunettes. Five degrees of erythema are recognized:

Suberythema — no visible subjective skin change 24 hours after exposure

Minimal erythema — moderate reddening of the skin 24 hours after exposure

First-degree erythema — moderate reddening of the skin 48 hours after exposure, followed by peeling of small patches of skin

Second-degree erythema — angry reddening of the skin lasting three days to a week, followed by peeling of large areas of skin in sheets

Third-degree erythema — angry reddening of the skin leading to blister formation and sloughing of epidermis and dermis. After healing, the area becomes darkly pigmented and remains so for from three to six months.

Indications for Use

Rickets (prevention as
  well as cure)
Infantile tetany or
  spasmophilia
Infected ulcers and
  wounds
Sluggish ulcers
  (for stimulation)
Dermatologic conditions
Minor burns
Mild degrees of calcium
  and phosphorus deficiency
  in children
Osteomalacia in pregnant or nursing women

Contraindications

Active and progressive
  forms of pulmonary
  tuberculosis
Advanced heart disease
  with failure of compensation
Advanced arteriosclerosis
Renal or hepatic
  insufficiency
Hyperthyroidism
Diabetes (may cause
  severe itching)
Generalized dermatitis

Special Precautions

The patient's sensitivity to ultraviolet should be determined by
the degree of erythema produced by ultraviolet radiation.

The eyes should be covered carefully with goggles or a wet
cotton pledget. If the eyes are merely closed and not covered by
cotton or cloth, the lids may become slightly edematous after
the treatment.

4
ELECTRICAL CURRENT

DIRECT (GALVANIC) CURRENT

Galvanic current is a form of direct current; it is steady, continuous, and unidirectional. This current can cause muscle contraction even though the nerve supply of the muscle is no longer intact. Consequently, galvanic current is used chiefly to produce muscular contractions. It may also be used to introduce medications consisting of inorganic compounds into and through the skin, and to overstimulate the sensory nerves, thus producing a transient reduction in response to stimuli.

Physiological and Chemical Effects

Galvanic current produces an increase in blood flow and tissue metabolism, thus relieving pain, and maintains muscle response to stimuli in peripheral nerve lesions while regeneration of the nerve takes place.

Galvanic current produces its effect by chemical action. As it passes through the body it breaks up the molecules it encounters into their composite atoms and ions. All ions possess either a positive or negative charge, and attract or repel each other. Like charges repel, unlike ones attract. When two dissimilar ions unite, they form a neutral molecule, but when galvanism breaks this union, they revert to positive and negative ions. At the point of entrance of galvanic current into the body a positive charge collects; at the point of exit a negative charge collects. The positive pole attracts negative and repels positive ions, while the negative pole attracts positive and repels negative ions. This is the reason for the importance of polarity in placing the electrode pads in the right place; if wrongly placed the results will be the reverse of what is desired. Therefore, one should be sure to understand the principle of polar action before treating a patient.

The following table lists the actions produced at the respective poles.

Positive pole	*Negative pole*
Attracts oxygen	Attracts hydrogen
Acid	Alkaline
Dehydrates tissues	Liquefies tissues
Vasoconstrictor	Vasodilator
Causes ischemia	Causes hyperemia
Stops bleeding	Causes bleeding
More germicidal	Less germicidal
Sedative	Stimulant
Repels bases, metals, alkaloids	Repels acid, acid radicals, halogens
Corrodes metals by oxidation	Does not corrode metals
Relieves pain in congestion	Causes pain (except in certain cases in which there is ischemia)

To determine polarity, one of the two following tests may be used:

1. Litmus paper test: Select a piece of litmus paper. With the current turned on, contact the paper with poles one half inch apart. Blue litmus paper will turn red under the positive pole. If the test is made with red litmus paper, the paper will turn blue under the negative pole.
2. Water test: Place both poles in a tumbler of water, being careful not to short the poles by contact with each other. Watch for bubbles; twice as many bubbles will collect at the negative pole as at the positive.

Suggested Techniques for Application

As will be generally recognized, the application of electrical current will depend upon the judgment and experience of the doctor in regard to the physical and chemical effects of the current employed.

The following suggestions are merely illustrative, and are based on the research and writing of authorities experienced in the use of electrical currents. It should be remembered that the physician in charge, having access to the patient's case history and the results of his examination, must assume responsibility for the treatment selected as well as for its application and its results.

As has been stated in the paragraph on the physiological effects of galvanic current, the current has to leave and enter the body through electrodes. In most instances, the effects to be obtained are desired under only one of the two electrodes. This electrode is then called the active electrode. The only function of the second electrode, which is called the dispersive electrode, is to complete the circuit and conduct the current either into or out of the body. While the shape and form of the active electrode vary from application to application, the dispersive electrode is more or less indifferent to the process, and the rules governing it are similar for all applications. The first and most important rule is that the dispersive electrode should be as large as is conveniently possible.

Electrodes should be well wetted. In large clinics and hospitals where electrical methods are used extensively, electrodes are often kept continuously wet. Soaking the electrodes, particularly large ones, for a few seconds or minutes results in unequal wetting and therefore in an unequal spread of the current over the electrodes. The placement of the dispersive electrode is relatively unimportant, except for the need of a large flat contact with the body surface. For instance, if a leg is treated, the placement of the dispersive electrode under the buttocks is preferable to placement under the shoulders. If the right arm is being treated, placement of the dispersive electrode under the right buttock or even on the same arm is recommended.

The correct placement of the negative and positive poles, proper strength of current, and length of treatment for specific conditions are as follows:

Adhesions

Negative pole: Larger wet-pad electrode placed over the plantar surface of either foot; if on the involved foot, make sure that the two electrodes do not meet

Positive pole: Smaller wet-pad electrode, saturated with 5% magnesium sulfate solution, placed over the involved ankle

Time: 10 to 15 minutes

Ankle Edema

Negative pole: Larger wet-pad electrode placed over the plantar surface of either foot; if on the involved foot, make sure that the two electrodes do not meet

Postive pole: Smaller wet-pad electrode, saturated with 5% magnesium sulfate solution, placed over the involved ankle

Current: 5 to 10 ma

Time: 15 to 30 minutes

Ankle Sprain, Acute

Negative pole: Smaller wet-pad electrode, saturated with 2% sodium salicylate, placed over the involved area

Positive pole: Larger wet-pad electrode placed on the upper third of the leg above the ankle being treated

Current: 1 to 3 ma

Time: 15 minutes

Ankle Sprain, Chronic

Negative pole: Smaller wet-pad electrode, saturated with 2% potassium iodide solution, placed over the involved area

Positive pole: Larger wet-pad electrode, placed over the calf of the leg above the ankle being treated

Current: 1 to 3 ma

Time: 15 minutes

Backache, Strain, or Fatigue

Negative pole: Wet-pad electrode (4 x 6 inches), placed opposite painful area

Positive pole: Wet-pad electrode (3 x 4 inches), saturated with 1% Novocain in 80% grain alcohol and placed over painful area

Current: 10 to 15 ma

Time: 15 minutes; subsequent treatments as required

Bruises

Negative pole: Smaller wet-pad electrode, well moistened, placed over the area to be treated

Positive pole: Larger wet-pad electrode placed on an area opposite the smaller negative electrode

Current: 2 to 10 ma

Time: 10 minutes

Bursitis

Negative pole: Smaller wet-pad electrode, well saturated with 2% sodium salicylate solution and placed on the area over the deltoid muscle

Positive pole: Larger wet-pad electrode placed over the upper thoracic spine

Current: 20 to 25 ma

Time: 25 to 30 minutes

Neuritis

Negative pole: Smaller wet-pad electrode, saturated with 2% sodium salicylate solution and placed over the area to be treated

Positive pole: Larger wet-pad electrode, well saturated, placed alongside the active electrode but not in contact with it

Current: 5 ma

Time: 10 to 15 minutes

Paralysis

The first step in the treatment of paralysis by galvanic current is for the therapist to ask the physician for a neuromuscular diagnosis of the patient's condition. If paresis is present in an isolated muscle, it is advisable to treat the muscle from motor point to tendon insertion in order to avoid escape of current to surrounding nonaffected muscles which may already be in a spastic or tetanized state.

The aim of treatment in paralysis is to create a feeling of contraction so that the patient may eventually duplicate that feeling by voluntary contraction. In all instances, treatment should be kept below the fatigue level. In advanced cases, intermittent current is used for the initial treatment and is followed by continuous pulsating direct current. Both currents provide the necessary increase in circulation and nutrition to the nerve and muscle. For optimum results, therapy must be continued for a considerable time.

Scar Tissue

Negative pole: Smaller wet-pad electrode, consisting of absorbent cotton or lint well saturated with 2% sodium chloride solution, placed over the scar tissue and covered with a small metal block

Positive pole: Larger wet-pad electrode placed at any convenient point, preferably opposite the location of the scar tissue being treated

Current: Regulated to a comfortable tolerance

Time: 30 minutes daily or every other day

Synovitis

Electrodes: Place negative and positive electrodes of equal size on the lateral and medial surfaces of the joint; these positions are reversed on subsequent treatment. The galvanic current hastens the absorption of accumulated fluids as it passes through the joint and produces quick results in both relief of pain and reduction of edema

Frequency of treatment: Daily

Iontophoresis

Iontophoresis is the introduction of a drug into the deeper layers of the skin by means of a low-amperage galvanic current. This procedure is also known as ion transfer. An active electrode is saturated with the required electrolytic solution, applied to the tissues, and connected to the positive pole of the direct current generator if positive ions are to be introduced, and to the negative pole if negative ions are to be used. The velocity of the ions employed and the circulating blood will limit the depth of penetration as well as the degree of concentration in the tissues.

Technique

A smooth galvanic current is the most suitable for administration of a drug by iontophoresis. Any form of galvanic current generator will do. The correct polarity of the two poles of the generator must be known and the electrodes must be connected to the proper terminals. For treatment through the skin, an active-pad electrode is made of absorbent material of sufficient thickness to hold the solution and to remain moist during treatment. A half-inch thickness of gauze is best, but cotton or felt of the same thickness is satisfactory. For the introduction of vasodilating drugs, blotting paper or special asbestos fabric paper is employed. The active electrode is soaked with the solution, which should be of comfortable warmth. The strength of the solution should be about 1%, but never higher than 2%. The saturated pad is laid on, with firm contact, over the area to be treated. A metal plate of somewhat smaller size is placed upon this pad carefully, so that the metal edge does not touch the bare skin, for it may cause a burn. (Treatment pads that are to be used again must be thoroughly cleansed and washed after each treatment in order to get rid of any secondary chemical products that might come into contact with the metal plate.)

Ions with a positive charge, such as zinc and copper, and such alkaloids as the vasodilating drugs are introduced into the skin and mucous membranes from the positive pole; ions with a negative charge, such as iodine, chlorine, and salicylates, are introduced into the tissues from the negative pole.

Treatment time and strength of current used will depend upon the substance used. For example:

Copper and zinc — 10 to 15 minutes; 5 to 15 ma
Histamine — 5 to 10 minutes; 5 to 10 ma
Mecholyl — up to 20 minutes; 20 to 30 ma
Procaine — up to 30 minutes; up to 30 ma

For procaine iontophoresis, which has been found to be a very useful modality, a solution of 1% procaine hydrochloride and 5 minims of Adrenalin 1/20,000 in 80% alcohol is used. The treatment area must be considerably larger than the area of pain distribution. A gauze pad is soaked in the solution and placed over the treatment area. A hand towel folded once or twice, soaked in saline, is then spread over the gauze, and a flexible metal electrode is placed over it. The positive pole of the galvanic current is attached to the metal electrode. A neutral electrode of approximately the same size, moistened with weak saline, is connected with the negative pole. A low-amperage current is applied to flow for 20 minutes. The area treated will show blanching. Surface analgesia will be present. Usually, two or three treatments will be sufficient; they should be given daily.

Indications for Use

For all forms of arthritis, ion transfer has been administered with salt, salicylates, lithium, iodine, histamine, and Mecholyl.

Histamine and saline ion transfer have been applied to sprains, synovitis, tenosynovitis, bursitis, fibrositis, myositis, and myalgia.

In peripheral vascular diseases, such as thromboangiitis obliterans, Raynaud's disease, and chronic phlebitis, histamine and Mecholyl are used.

Certain diseases of the nervous system, such as trigeminal neuralgia, have been treated similarly. Neuritis has been treated with ordinary salt solution and also with local anesthetics such as cocaine and Nupercaine. Saline iontophoresis has been used for neuralgic conditions such as hemiplegia.

Diseases of the skin offer good opportunities for ion transfer. Fungus diseases are treated successfully with such drugs as silver nitrate and copper sulfate.

Magnesium sulfate iontophoresis has been used for relaxation of muscle spasticity such as occurs in hemiplegia.

Very good results have been obtained with the use of procaine iontophoresis, followed by active exercise, in the treatment of sprains, bursitis, low back pain, sciatica, chronic shoulder spasm, and other spasm of muscular origin.

Special Points to Remember When Using Galvanic Current in Physical Therapy

The results obtained in all physical therapy applications of electricity are in proportion to the exactness with which they are applied. The following suggestions will help to make the application of galvanic current a success:

1. Explain the treatment to the patient in detail, i.e., the sensation and results to be expected.
2. The connecting wires should be well insulated and checked for any defects in insulation. Naked wires and connectors should not be allowed to come into contact with the patient's body.
3. Electrode plugs should be thoroughly checked for quality of contact. When strong galvanic current is being applied, the sudden interruption of the current can produce a very unpleasant shock.
4. Galvanic current treatment should not be given on a metal table because of the possibility of contact of the wet electrode with the table.
5. The skin to which electrodes are to be applied should be thoroughly cleansed of adhesive tape and medication before starting treatment. Scars should be protected.
6. Protect the patient's clothing from getting soiled.
7. Use the right pole in the right place.
8. Make sure the electrodes are proportionately the right size.
9. Never attempt to use dry metal electrodes when applying galvanic current.

10. Never apply a lubricant to metal electrodes used in galvanic-current treatments.

11. Wet-pad electrodes should be thoroughly soaked in warm water before using. They should be wet almost to the point of dripping.

12. Study the affected parts and see that the pads are properly placed.

13. Start the current at low intensity; increase the intensity gradually.

14. Avoid creating shocks, i.e., picking up or changing pads, reversing polarity, etc., while the current is turned on.

15. Do not overdo the first treatment.

16. If the patient complains of a stinging sensation under the wet pad electrodes, there is probably a dry spot on the electrode — a problem easily remedied by additional moistening of the electrode; or there may be an abrasion of the skin or scar tissue.

17. The therapist should at all times realize that the patient is actually part of the electrical circuit. In the application of direct current, the increase in amperage should always be gradual, and it should be an automatic rule to reduce the amperage control to the zero position at the end of the treatment.

18. Galvanic current used for destruction of superfluous hair or small growths should be administered by a physician.

ALTERNATING CURRENT

The two types of alternating current employed in physical therapy are faradic current and the sinusoidal-wave current.

Faradic Current

Faradic current is a form of alternating current that constantly changes direction. It consists of two pulses in opposite directions which follow each other immediately. One of the pulses is of high intensity and very short duration and the pulse in the opposite direction is of longer duration and lower intensity. The polarity effects of the current while flowing in one direction are thus opposed by those flowing in the opposite direction, with the result that the polarization effects are of little importance. The strength of a faradic current is regulated by varying the relative distance between the primary and secondary coil. Sliding the secondary coil over the primary increases the strength of the current by inductive power. When faradic stimulation is applied either to the motor point or anywhere along a nerve, the intervals between current flow are too short to permit relaxation of the muscles. A contraction results. The physiologic effect of this current stimulation of muscles differs very little from that obtained by other forms of electrical stimulation. The faradic method of accomplishing muscular contractions, however, differs from that of other types of electrical stimulation currents. The effective phase of the secondary faradic current occurs at the break. The break phases are very rapid, up to 100 times per second. At this rate of speed, the break stimuli follow one another so rapidly that muscles with a normal nerve supply have no time to relax and a smooth tetanus occurs. The amount of sensation produced by the faradic current depends chiefly on the duration of each individual break of current flow. If it is short, there is no sensation of pain, but if it is long there will be pain. A flow of current for 1/1000th of a second is capable of causing contraction of a muscle with a normal nerve, but is incapable of producing contraction in a paralyzed muscle. However, a paralyzed muscle still possesses the ability of any muscle to respond to sufficiently long electrical stimulation, but, because of its lack of innervation, the muscle does not respond to an electrical current stimulus that lasts for only 1/1000th of a second. This cardinal point is the reason for the use of this type of current in muscle testing.

Indications for Use

A normal muscle with a normal nerve will respond to faradic stimulation, but if there is damage or injury to the nerve in that muscle, there will be no response to this type of current. This type of current, therefore, is used in the following conditions:

1. To stimulate muscles that are poor in tone but have a normal nerve.
2. To test for the presence of reaction of degeneration (see p. 35).

Sinusoidal-wave Current

The sinusoidal-wave current is a uniform, continuous-wave type of alternating current. In using this current for physical therapy treatment, the voltage can be increased gradually from zero to whatever voltage is desired and then allowed to recede gradually through the zero mark until it reaches a negative point equal to its previous rise. Then it returns to zero again. This complete operation is called a cycle, and the sinusoidal-wave current is a continuous repetition of these cycles. Each cycle contains an exactly equal amount of positive and negative electricity, and is, therefore, neutral as far as chemical action is concerned. The sinusoidal wave-current creates a muscular contraction with each impulse. The duration of the treatment therefore, should not be too long or it will result in a tiring of the muscles. No attention need be paid to the respective poles; they are equal in electrical output. The smallest electrode will be the one of greatest activity for localized applications. The difference in pad sizes applies to the sinusoidal currents as it does to galvanism (see p. 25).

Sinusoidal-wave currents may be rapid, with alternations of 40 to 80 cycles per second and impulses lasting about 1/100th of a second, or slow, with 5 to 30 cycles per second and single impulses lasting about 1/50th of a second or longer.

ELECTRODIAGNOSIS

Electrodiagnosis is a means of determining the nature of muscle and nerve pathology by observing changes in electrical irritability of these tissues. It is a valuable aid from the standpoint of diagnosis, prognosis, and prescription for therapy in pathological conditions of the motor tract, including the brain, the spinal cord, and the peripheral nerves, as well as the muscles.

Strong electrical current applied to any muscular part of the body will cause disagreeable shocks and muscular jerks over a widespread area. But a single muscle or specific muscular area, if it is normal and undamaged, will respond to a minimal stimulus by application of electrical current. It is important to remember this, because if there is injury or damage to the nerve in a particular muscle, there will be no response to electrical stimuli.

Muscle Testing with Galvanic Current

Galvanic current exerts a stimulating effect on nerves and muscles through sudden and gradual chemical changes in the tissues. When an electrical current of a constant (unchanging) strength flows through a muscle or nerve-muscle preparation, no visible contraction occurs. Only when the current is suddenly "started" ("made") at sufficient strength, or when its flow is interrupted ("broken") while flowing, will visible muscular contraction occur.

The "make" and "break" of galvanic current (also known as interrupted galvanic current) furnish the simplest means for testing the reaction, or muscle stimulation, when single contractions are desirable. Therefore, galvanic current is a useful diagnostic tool for: (1) stimulating muscles that are poor in tone but have a normal nerve, and (2) testing for the presence of reaction to degeneration.

Significance of the Reaction of Degeneration (RD)

The importance of the reaction of degeneration (RD) to prognosis lies in the fact that, if it is present 10 days after an injury or after a disease process starts, changes in nerve and muscle substance will require considerable time — several months at least — to recover. However, the finding of RD by no means indicates that the damage is irreparable.

The occurrence of RD proves the presence of a lesion of a lower motor neuron of the nervous system, consisting of the anterior horn cell, anterior root and nerve plexuses, and peripheral nerve. Clinically, such a lesion is always accompanied by flaccid paralysis and loss of tendon reflexes.

Motor Points

Every muscle, unless deeply covered by other muscles, possesses a small area where it is most easily excited and which will respond with visible contraction when stimulated electrically. This is called the *motor point*. It is usually located near the origin of the muscle belly, where the nerve enters the muscle. Trigger point scanning is often a very helpful diagnostic tool in finding the motor point of a particular muscle. Scanning is done by passing an electrode over the areas indicated in the diagrams below. The areas scanned for locating the motor points of certain muscles are shown in outline; the motor points are marked with an X. (Reproduced by permission of the Iowa State Department of Health from their publication, *The Physical Therapy Manual for Physicians*.)

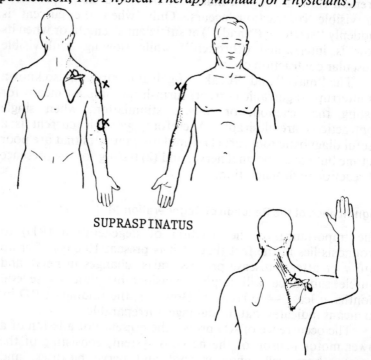

SUPRASPINATUS

LEVATOR SCAPULAE

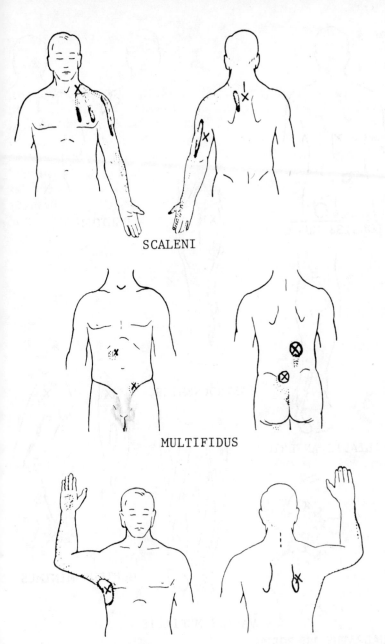

SCALENI

MULTIFIDUS

SUBSCAPULARIS AND SERRATUS ANTERIOR

37

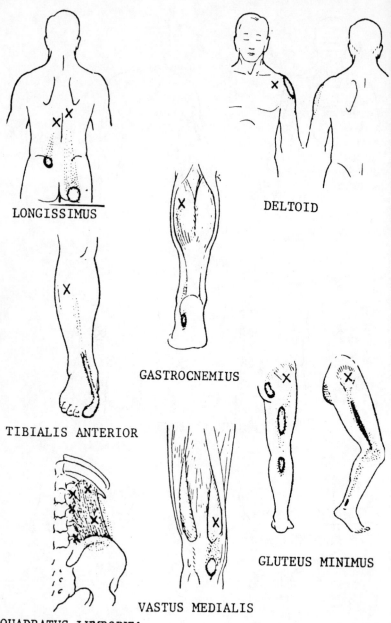

LONGISSIMUS

DELTOID

GASTROCNEMIUS

TIBIALIS ANTERIOR

GLUTEUS MINIMUS

VASTUS MEDIALIS

QUADRATUS LUMBORUM

38

Figure 1. The seven motor point charts which follow were furnished by courtesy of the Burdick Corporation, Milton, Wisconsin (copyright 1955) and are reprinted with their permission. Certain changes in lettering were made to accommodate each chart without undue reduction in size. As there are many anatomical variations, the charts have been standardized in a reasonable manner. The following abbreviations are used: M–Muscle; N–Nerve; B–Branch of Nerve; C–Cervical Nerve Roots; T–Thoracic Nerve Roots; L–Lumbar Nerve Roots. Numbers refer to innervation and are explained for each chart individually.

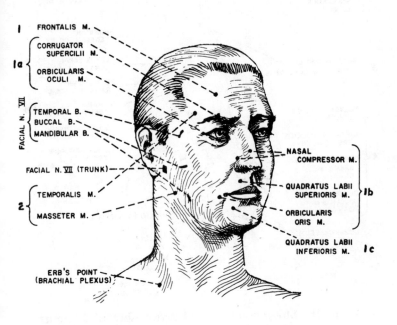

Figure 1a. Motor points of the face

1. Facial N. VII
1a. Facial N. VII, temporal and zygomatic branches
1b. Facial N. VII, buccal branch
1c. Facial N. VII, mandibular and buccal branches
2. Trigeminus N.

39

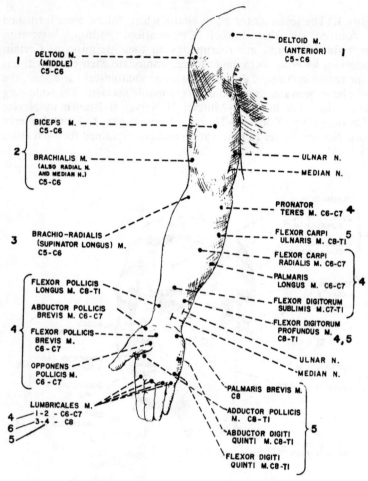

Figure 1b. Motor points of the anterior aspect of the upper extremity

1. Axillary N. (Circumflex N.)
2. Musculocutaneous N.
3. Radial N.
4. Median N.
5. Ulnar N.
6. Ulnar N., or mixed Median and Ulnar N., or Median N.

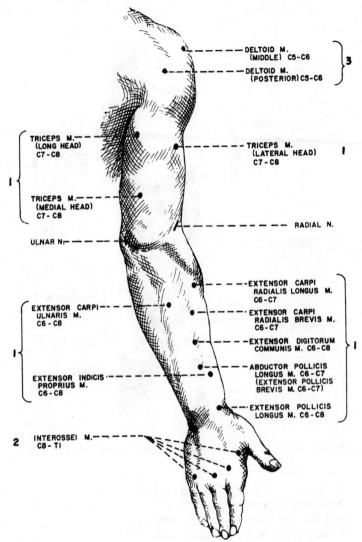

Figure 1c. Motor points of the posterior aspect of the upper extremity

1. Radial N.
2. Ulnar N.
3. Axillary N. (Circumflex N.)

41

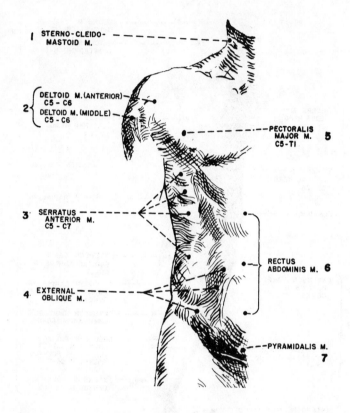

Figure 1d. Motor points of the anterior aspect of the trunk

1. Spinal Accessory N. XI and C2-C3
2. Axillary N. (Circumflex N.)
3. Long Thoracic N. (Brachial Plexus)
4. Intercostal N. 8-12, Ilioninguinal N. LI, Iliohypogastric
5. Medial and Lateral Anterior Thoracic N. (Brachial Plexus)
6. Intercostal N. 7-12
7. 12th Thoracic N.

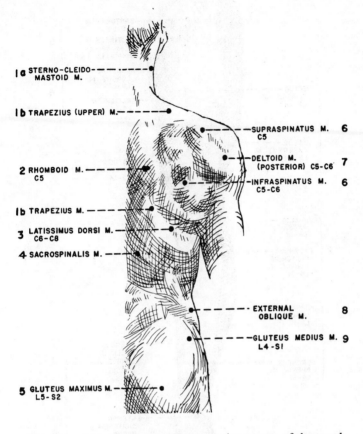

Figure 1e. Motor points of the posterior aspect of the trunk

1a. Spinal Accessory N. XI and C2-C3
1b. Spinal Accessory N. XI and C3-C4
2. Dorsal Scapular N. (Brachial Plexus)
3. Thoracodorsal N. (Brachial Plexus)
4. Posterior Rami of Thoracic N. and Lumbar N.
5. Inferior Gluteal N.
6. Suprascapular N.
7. Axillary N. (Circumflex N.)
8. Intercostal N. 8-12, Iliohypogastric N. LI, and
   Ilioninguinal N. LI
9. Superior Gluteal N.

43

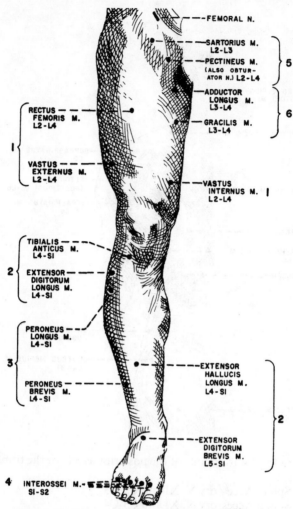

Figure 1f. Motor points of the anterior aspect of the lower exremity

1. Femoral N.
2. Deep Peroneal N.
3. Superficial Peroneal N.
4. Lateral Plantar N. (Branch of Tibial N.)
5. Femoral Crural N.
6. Obturator N.

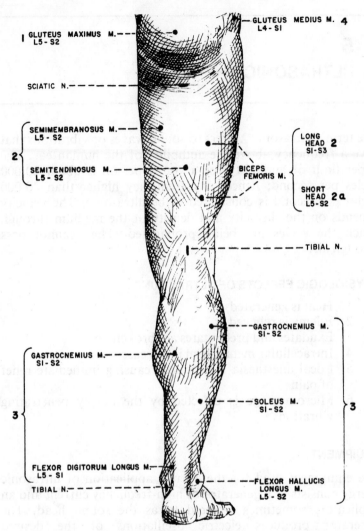

Figure 1g. Motor points of the posterior aspect of the lower extremity

1. Inferior Gluteal N.
2. Tibial Portion of Sciatic N. or Tibial N.
2a. Peroneal Portion of Sciatic N. or Peroneal N.
3. Tibial N.
4. Superior Gluteal N.

45

5
ULTRASONIC THERAPY

The term "ultrasonic" refers to sound waves or vibrations that have a frequency above the audibility of the human ear. The upper limit of audibility for a young person is about 20,000 cycles per second; hence, any frequency higher than 20,000 cycles per second is considered to be ultrasonic. The velocity depends on the elasticity and density of the medium through which the waves are being propagated. They cannot pass through air.

PHYSIOLOGIC EFFECTS OF ULTRASOUND

1. Heat is generated
2. Edema is relieved
3. Exudates and precipitates are broken up
4. Intracellular metabolism is increased
5. Local anesthesia is produced causing immediate relief of pain
6. Micromassage is effected by the deeply penetrating vibrations

EQUIPMENT

The equipment used for therapeutic application of ultrasonic energy consists of a generator of high-frequency current and an applicator, sometimes referred to as the sound head. The generator produces electric oscillations of the desired frequency, which cause the transducer in the applicator to vibrate and generate sound waves. This sonic energy is transmitted to human tissue by contact with the applicator face.

METHODS AND TECHNIQUES OF APPLICATION

Since ultrasonic radiations cannot pass through air, an air-free contact must be established between the applicator and the tissue. This is accomplished by providing a coupling medium between the applicator and the skin, such as mineral oil or water. If oil is used, it is applied to the skin over the area to be treated and the face of the applicator is moved over the skin with light pressure; for larger areas it is applied with stroking movements and for smaller areas with a circular movement. Water coupling is a convenient method for treating extremities; when water is used, both the body part and the face of the applicator are immersed. When this underwater technique is employed, the applicator is kept 1 to 2 centimeters away from the skin and slowly moved in a circular manner. The purpose of moving the sound head is to insure uniform distribution of energy and obviate the necessity for pinpointing accurately small targets such as nerves, ganglia, or blood vessels.

As the sound waves travel through the tissue, part of the energy of motion is transformed into heat. This heat can penetrate to a depth of 5 centimeters or more. In more or less homogeneous tissue, the heating will be fairly uniform. This has been referred to as volume heating. When the ultrasonic rays are impeded by interfaces in tissue, such as exist between bone and muscle, increased localized heating takes place in the region of the interface. This has been termed structural heating. This localized heating at interfaces produced by ultrasonic radiation is not produced by any other form of heat therapy.

In summary, it may be said that tissue heating by ultrasound can be accomplished with good depth of penetration and with maximum absorption by muscle tissue. The good beaming characteristics of ultrasound radiation permit better localization than afforded by other forms of heat therapy.

DOSAGE

At present there is no established dosage for ultrasonic therapy, but the dosage for therapeutic purposes should be limited. Ultrasound dosage depends on intensity and time, and the product of these factors is usually expressed as watt-minutes. Intensity of sound energy available from the sound head (transducer) is usually expressed as watts per square centimeter of the energized surface. Therapeutic intensities of 0.5 to 2.0

watts per square centimeter have been found useful. Underwater treatment demands greater treatment intensities because of absorption and reflection of the waves by the medium. Treatment time is progressive, beginning at 5 minutes and increasing to a maximum of 8 to 10 minutes per treatment area. A treatment series is considered to be 6 to 12 applications, applied daily according to some authorities, every other day according to others.

In determining dosage it will be useful to remember that acute conditions require low intensity treatment, and chronic ones require stimulation provided from higher intensities. Deep-seated lesions need initial high intensity treatment.

Much can be observed from the patient's reaction during treatment. He should feel no pain or discomfort. A sense of burning, tingling, or pain indicates that the treatment dosage is too intense. (Because of the localized heating at interfaces there may be pain in the bony areas without discomfort to the skin.) This may result from either (1) not moving the treatment head fast enough, i.e., staying too long in one spot and building up intensity; or (2) too great a power output. In the first case, the remedy is to move the sound head away from the area of discomfort; in the second, to reduce the power setting of the generator. Pain may be considered the natural line of defense against too high dosages. In general, it is well to begin with low dosages and increase progressively in time and intensity.

INDICATIONS FOR USE

In some clinics and hospitals ultrasonic therapy is utilized in combination with such other physical therapy modalities as infrared radiation, diathermy, and whirlpool baths.

Investigators and clinicians have used ultrasound therapy for the following conditions:

Bursitis	Periarthritis
Fibrositis	Radiculitis
Osteoarthritis	Rheumatoid arthritis
Painful neuroma	Scars

CONTRAINDICATIONS

Although ultrasonic therapy is considered a safe form of treatment, it should not be used in conditions that are aggravated by it or for treatment of diseases that are known to respond to other modes of treatment.

Some authorities have advised against the use of ultrasonics directly over the brain, eye, middle and inner ear, reproductive organs, visceral plexuses, and large automatic ganglia.

Sounding of the heart and stellate ganglion should be avoided in patients with heart disease.

Caution should be exercised when considering the use of ultrasonics for patients with malignancies, since stimulation of growth of the primary tumor and even metastases have been reported after its application.

6
HYDROTHERAPY

The use of water in treating disease is an ancient practice and still has many uses for various pathological conditions. Water may have diaphoretic, diuretic, emetic, hypnotic, purgative, sedative, or stimulating effects. It may be used hot, warm, cold, or in the form of ice. All or part of the body may be treated. The pathological condition for which it is prescribed will determine the type of hydrotherapy used and the method of application.

BATHS

Many different types of baths are used in physical therapy. Substances that are sometimes added to the bath for their therapeutic effects include mustard, starch, bran, oatmeal, sodium bicarbonate, sulfur, tar, salt, and potassium permanganate.

Cold Bath

Cold water baths are sometimes ordered for their stimulating effect. When of short duration they increase muscle tone and energy; produce pallor of the skin and contraction of the cutaneous fibers, causing "goose pimples" followed by reddening of the skin; diminish the heart rate and lengthen the period of diastole; raise the blood pressure; cause peripheral vessels to contract as the blood is driven into deeper regions; cause the patient to gasp and breathe deeply; increase metabolism and amount of oxygen inspired; and impart a refreshing sensation. Cold baths of long duration produce stiffness, shivering, and diminished functional capacity.

Warm Bath

Warm water baths of short duration tend to lessen fatigue and irritability and cause relaxation of the muscles. When prolonged, however, they have an enervating effect. They also stimulate the sweat glands, dilate the peripheral blood vessels and so increase slightly the work of the heart, lower the blood pressure, cause the patient to gasp (but not as deeply as cold baths), increase the metabolic rate if the bath is hot enough and the patient remains in it for a long time, and relieve pain more effectively than cold baths.

Tepid Sponge Bath

The tepid sponge bath serves to promote relaxation, relieve discomfort, stimulate circulation, and temporarily reduce a high fever. One part of the body at a time should be sponged with water at a temperature of about 80° F, and lightly dried. It is imperative to avoid chilling the patient; the room should be warm and free from drafts, and covers should be used judiciously. The water bath should be followed by sponging with a 25% alcohol solution warmed to 105° F.

Hot Sitz Bath

The hot sitz bath may be used for relief of pain in prostatitis, hemorrhoids, dysmenorrhea, and coccygodynia.

A washtub may be used for home treatment; special sitz bath equipment will be found in hospitals. Water should reach the level of the patient's umbilicus when he is sitting in the tub with his legs outside. Water should be at a temperature of 98° to 104°F; duration of the bath should be from 15 to 30 minutes. The patient's chest and shoulders should be covered with a blanket and his feet and legs wrapped in a separate blanket.

Contrast Bath

Contrast baths consist of sudden and alternate immersions of the extremities in first hot and then cold water. Two containers are used, each large enough to accommodate both arms or both legs. The hot water should be kept at a temperature of 105° to 110°F, and the cold water at 60° to 65°F. (For diabetics, the hot water temperature must be lowered to 105°F.)

One should start the bath by immersing the part or parts to be treated in hot water for 10 minutes. Then the part is transferred immediately to the cold water for 1 minute, then back to the hot water for 1 minute, and then to cold water again for 1 minute. This 3-minute cycle is repeated for the prescribed length of time every 20 to 30 minutes, always being preceded by the 10-minute hot water phase.

Physiological Effects

Contrast baths cause an intense vascular reaction that greatly stimulates peripheral circulation through active contraction and relaxation of the blood vessels.

Indications for Use

Arthritis
Chilblains
Contusions
Fractures
To toughen amputation stumps

Contraindications

Loss of sensation of heat and/or cold
Arterial insufficiency
Advanced arteriosclerosis

Whirlpool Bath

The equipment used for the whirlpool bath is a specially manufactured vessel of suitable size to accommodate an arm or leg (sometimes the entire body), with water delivered at high temperatures and mixed with air by hydrostatic pressure or by an electric mixer. The equipment can be made by a good local plumber. The temperature of the water, controlled by .a thermostatic valve, is usually started at 100°F and increased to the patient's tolerance. Baths are usually of 20 to 25 minutes duration and may be given twice a day.

Indications for Use

Acute arthritis
Adherent, painful scars
Adhesions
Burns
Cicatrices (painful, adherent)
Decubitus ulcers
Fractures, after casts
   have been bivalved
   or removed
Hematoma
Indolent ulcers
Ischemic contracture
Legs freed from
   long immobilization
Low back pain
Nerve injuries

Painful amputation
   stumps
Peripheral nerve
   lesions, acute
   stage
Peripheral vascular
   diseases, early stages
Purulent wounds
Sprains, subacute
Strains, subacute
Synovitis
Tendon repairs,
   3 to 4 weeks
   after surgery
Tenosynovitis, subacute
Varicose veins, chronic

Hubbard Tub Bath

The Hubbard tub (or tank) is used chiefly for the administration of underwater exercises and for the relief of muscle pain and spasm; it is also sometimes very useful in treating certain orthopedic conditions.

It may be necessary to employ an overhead crane to lift the patient into the tub for treatment. In some institutions, a canvas stretcher is used in conjunction with the crane. The patient is placed on the stretcher, which is then lifted by means of four cables that extend from the crane to the four corners of the stretcher; moved into position over the tub; and lowered into the water, which is maintained at 95° to 104°F. Sometimes the cables are then detached, sometimes not.

While the patient is in the tub (or tank), a backrest or head support is adjusted so that he can lie in the water comfortably and still move his arms and legs freely. The physical therapist or aide stands at the side of the tub to direct and assist the patient with various types of exercise as indicated. Duration of treatment is usually 20 to 25 minutes.

Indications for Use

Arthritis (generalized, involving many joints)
Burns (especially when contractures have developed)
Dislocations (after reduction)
Fractures of vertebrae, pelvis, or femur
Neuritis, selected forms
Paresis of upper and lower extremities
Tendon repair or transplant, upon termination of immobilization

Contraindications

Extreme age and senility

WET COMPRESS

Wet compresses, either hot or cold, may be used on various parts of the body and for various purposes.

Cold Wet Compress

Cold wet compresses to the head are useful to lessen febrile headache and usually accompany other hydrotherapeutic procedures for fever. A Turkish towel is wrung out of ice water and applied to the head like a turban. An ice bag may be applied over it.

Cold throat compresses are useful in tonsillitis and laryngitis. Two strips of linen 3 inches wide and long enough to reach under the chin from one ear to the other are immersed in water at 60°F, wrung out, and placed on a piece of flannel 3½ inches wide and long enough to reach around the head. The flannel strip is drawn together tightly on top of the head and fastened with safety pins. It is changed when it becomes warm and dry.

The trunk compress is a useful form of cold compress. It can be used for children and collapsed patients, and between other more radical procedures when the fever reaches very high levels. For an adult a sheet is used and for a child a Turkish towel; this is folded so as to fit over the trunk from the axilla to the pubis. It is wrung out of water at 60° to 70°F, wrapped snugly around the body, covered with a piece of dry flannel of the same size, and secured by safety pins. It is changed every 2 hours for fever above 104°F and every hour for fever above 105°F.

Hot Wet Compress

Hot wet compresses are applied in many conditions. The hot moist dressing is especially useful in treating spreading infections. A large sterile dressing is put around the infected part and moistened, not saturated, with a warm sterile solution. A thick, dry sterile pad is placed over it and heat from an electric room heater, an electric lamp, or an infrared lamp applied. Every 2 hours the outside covering is opened and the dressing is moistened with the sterile solution. Once every 24 hours the dressing is removed entirely and replaced, using careful sterile technique, by a fresh one.

The hot fomentation compress is useful in treatment of lumbago, sciatica, and bursitis. Two pieces of blanket, about 18 inches square, and a wringer constructed from a large towel with sticks inserted in slots in the ends, are needed. The wringer is placed in a basin and the blanket pieces laid on it. Boiling water is poured over these until they are saturated. The blanket pieces are wrung out until all hot water is expelled by twisting the sticks of the towel wringer in opposite directions. Make sure no drops of free water remain in the blanket compress, or burns will be produced. A folded dry blanket is placed under the affected part, and the skin is covered with vaseline. The blanket compresses are slipped out of the wringer and placed upon the area to be treated. The dry blanket is then brought around the body over the compresses, which are renewed every 15 minutes.

Moist Hot Pack

The moist hot pack is perhaps the most widely used physical therapy modality. For details see pages 11–13.

7
APPLICATION OF COLD

The application of cold, including ice, is a frequently used modality in physical therapy. Muscles constantly produce heat. When muscles are exposed to cold, there is need for increased production of heat and, subsequently, muscle tone is increased. Brief exposure to cold, therefore, causes an increase in work output. It also raises the stimulus threshold of muscle spindles and prolongs relaxation.

PHYSIOLOGICAL EFFECTS

The physiological effects of the local application of cold are many. Brief application produces no significant change in blood pressure. There is, however, an immediate constriction of the peripheral vessels of the skin, which drives the blood into the deeper vessels by a reflex action of the central nervous system. Whether the application of cold, at least local application, affects respiration is a controversial point. Some authorities claim that cold increases the basal and functional rate of metabolism.

In addition to the physiological effects of cold, cold therapy has the following advantages: it relieves muscle spasm and pain, reduces swelling, combines effectively with muscle reeducation that utilizes proprioceptive neuromuscular facilitation techniques, does not increase the risk of hemorrhage in acute trauma or muscle and ligament strain, diminishes spasticity and fatigue, and increases the patient's ability to perform voluntary motion.

Disadvantages of the local application of cold include the facts that it causes some degree of discomfort and that geriatric patients often cannot tolerate the therapy.

PROCEDURES FOR APPLICATION

1. Packs soaked in water at a temperature of 40°F are applied to the skin; they are changed every 45 minutes.
2. Turkish towels, soaked in water and shaved ice at a temperature of 58°F (or colder) are applied directly to the part involved.
3. Upper or lower limbs or hands or feet that are to be treated are immersed in a bath of ice and water at a temperature of 34°F. This may be painful at the start, and the part may be withdrawn after 20 to 30 seconds. The action is repeated several times over approximately 4 minutes.
4. Cold packs may be used alternately with heat on an affected part.
5. The spray technique employs a fluoromethane mixture in a pressure pack spray that is held about 18 inches from the skin while the mixture is sprayed directly on the part for about 3 seconds; this is repeated twice at intervals of 30 seconds.
6. The cryokinetic technique combines cold and motion. It employs ice massage, which is terminated when the part is sufficiently anesthetized to permit voluntary movement through the desirable range.
7. "Quick ice" (1 second) or "maintained ice" (3 seconds) applied to specific muscles provides external stimulation of the anterior horn cells to maintain muscle tone.

TESTS FOR REACTIONS TO COLD

The patient's reaction to the application of cold may be tested by using either the Baruch test or the wrapped forearm test. In the Baruch test, the physical therapist scratches across the patient's chest with his fingernail. If the area turns white, then quickly red, the patient's reactive capacity is within normal limits; if it remains white, the wrapped forearm test should be used. In this test, the forearm is wrapped in a towel that has been dipped in cold water and the arm is rubbed briskly for 20 seconds. Then the skin is checked; if it is red, the patient's reactive capacity is within normal limits; if it is white, the patient's reactive capacity is to be questioned.

INDICATIONS FOR USE

Low back sprains (early)
Whiplash injuries (early)
Painful cervical disorders
Painful shoulder (bursitis, for example)
For prestretching muscles
For relaxation of muscle spasm in patients who have had a cerebrovascular accident
Traumatic injuries to the central nervous system, including the spinal cord

CONTRAINDICATIONS

Impaired circulation
Peripheral vascular disease
Loss of thermal sensitivity
Psychological opposition to this type of therapy

8
PARAFFIN BATH

PHYSIOLOGICAL EFFECTS

A paraffin bath may be employed to keep a part to be treated warm and moist for a considerable length of time, thus making the skin soft, pliable, and ready for various physical therapy procedures such as massage and manipulation.

The ordinary commercial paraffin sold in grocery stores and used by housewives for sealing jelly jars is suitable for therapeutic paraffin baths. The paraffin is melted in a double boiler, a 1-½ quart size being convenient for most purposes. To avoid the danger of applying melted paraffin when it is too hot, temperatures should be checked with a thermometer. More simply, the paraffin may be cooled until the surface begins to congeal, which occurs at 125° to 130°F. The temperature of the paraffin bath may be lowered by mixing mineral oil with the solid paraffin in the ratio of one part mineral oil to four parts paraffin.

The area to which the paraffin is to be applied is washed clean and dried. If the hand is to be treated, it is rapidly immersed in the melted paraffin six to eight times, until a thick coating forms. At first contact the paraffin feels hot. However, on reimmersion of the hand, covered with the initial layer of paraffin, the sensation of heat is decidedly diminished. After several layers have been applied, the coating of paraffin looks like a thick glove. The hand can either be held in the melted paraffin from 20 to 30 minutes, or it can be removed, with the paraffin glove permitted to remain in place for about a half hour. After the paraffin has been removed the hand will be very red, moist, and soft — a condition suitable for massage or manipulation.

The advantages of using a paraffin bath before certain physical therapy procedures can easily be seen; a side benefit is that it can be adapted for use at home. However, it is a messy treatment, and somewhat malodorous, and debris from the skin accumulates in the paraffin. The paraffin can be cleansed of debris as follows: (1) melt it and strain it through fine gauze, or (2) boil it in two pints of water for 10 minutes and allow it to cool and set, which will cause dirt and debris to settle to the bottom for convenient removal. The latter method is said to be effective in killing bacteria and spore-forming organisms. Discard the paraffin about twice a year, depending on how often it has been used.

INDICATIONS FOR USE

Traumatic and other types of arthritis
Bursitis
Tenosynovitis
Stiff joints following fracture
Weakness and stiffness following nerve injuries
Scar tissue that results in limitation of motion

CONTRAINDICATIONS

Inability of the patient to tolerate heat, as occurs in certain neurological diseases and circulatory disturbances
Dermatologic disorders
Damaged or broken skin

9
MASSAGE

Massage is one of the oldest, most useful, and easily administered forms of treatment used for the relief of pain and other symptoms of disease and injury.

PHYSIOLOGICAL EFFECTS

The blood supply to a part is increased

The lymphatic and venous return is increased

Drainage from the region of an involved joint is hastened, thus decreasing periarticular swelling

Muscular relaxation is produced

Fibrosis and the formation of adhesions in muscles are prevented

The tendency for muscles to atrophy is decreased

TYPES OF MASSAGE

Effleurage

The aim of effleurage — superficial stroking toward the body or heart, using a slow, gentle, rhythmic movement — is to produce only a reflex action. To secure this effect, the pressure must be extremely light and each movement must be repeated in the same direction. Approximately 12 to 15 strokes per minute is the usual rate. The most common mistakes made by therapists are scratching the patient's skin with the fingertips near the end of each stroke, breaking the rhythm in the intervals between the strokes, and changing the direction of the strokes.

Stroking can be performed in four different ways:

1. *With one hand*: used upon the extremities, back of the head, and in single massage of the neck

2. *With both hands*: used upon the lower extremities of adults, upon the chest and back, and also in double massage of the neck

3. *With the thumb*: used between two muscles or between a muscle and a tendon, and frequently to reach the interossei of the hands and feet

4. *With the tips of the fingers*: used principally around the joints (in sprains, etc.), the fingers conforming themselves to the shape of the part to be worked upon

Deep Stroking

Deep stroking — stroking in the direction of the natural flow of lymph and venous blood — is aimed at emptying veins and lymphatics and pressing their contents in the direction of natural flow. It is essential to have the patient's muscles relaxed, to take advantage of gravity, to make the movements deep but not heavy, and to make them always in the direction of the venous flow.

Petrissage

The aim of petrissage — kneading by grasping, wringing, lifting, or pressing a part — is to assist venous and lymphatic circulation, to stretch retracted muscles and tendons, and to aid in stretching adhesions. The essentials in kneading massage are the same as those for deep stroking massage. One or both hands may be employed.

Friction

The effects of friction — pressing deeply on a part and moving the hand in a circular direction — are to free adherent skin, to loosen scars and adhesions of deeper parts, and to aid in the absorption of local effusion. Friction is an important type of massage to use around joints for small areas such as the hands, feet, and face. Friction massage may be given with the thumb, the tips of the fingers, or with one hand.

Tapotement (Percussion)

Tapotement, — or percussion, consists of striking the part quickly with the hand. Four types of percussion are used: (1) clapping with the palms of the hands, (2) hacking with the ulnar borders of the hands, (3) tapping with the tips of the fingers, and (4) beating with the clenched fist.

INDICATIONS FOR USE

Massage has many therapeutic uses and values. It is often prescribed for the following conditions:

Arthritis: to prevent or delay atrophy, to improve local and general metabolism, to improve circulation, and to relieve edema; it should be preceded by the application of heat and followed by exercise

Fibrositis: to break up nodules; very heavy massage of the friction type is required

Facial paralysis

Sprains

Contusions

Sacroiliac strain

Preparation of an amputation stump for use

Many orthopedic conditions, including back conditions

Neurologic disorders and nerve injuries

CONTRAINDICATIONS

Acutely inflamed joints

Phlebitis or lymphangiitis (because of danger of embolism)

Increased pain, swelling, or stiffness in a joint (persisting for more than two hours) following massage

Burns

Acute dermatitis

Suspected local malignancy

Suspected osteomyelitis or tuberculous lesion of bone

Presence of intra-abdominal tumor

Infection

Advanced arteriosclerosis

Advanced nephritis

10
CERVICAL TRACTION

Continuous traction assures a certain amount of immobilization of the cervical spine and relieves muscle spasm. When correctly applied, it straightens the cervical spine and enlarges the intervertebral foramina to relieve compressive or irritative forces upon the nerve roots. However, the conventional method of application by use of a head halter is not well tolerated because of the discomfort to the chin and lower jaw. Also, the conventional 5 to 10 pounds of weight does nothing more than lift the weight of the head from the neck and keep the patient still to some extent.

Intermittent traction, hand controlled or motorized, is supplanting all other methods of traction application (except, of course, skeletal or skull traction). Intermittent traction relieves muscle spasm because of its massage-like effect upon the muscles and the ligamentous and capsular structures. It reduces swelling, improves circulation in the tissues, and prevents the formation of adhesions between the dural sleeves of the nerve roots and the adjacent capsular structures. In some chronic conditions in which adhesions have been present for some time, intermittent traction may aggravate the symptoms of nerve root irritation because of the tug it places upon the adherent nerve roots. In such a case, the traction should be discontinued. The most advantageous intermittent traction is that which can be controlled in amount and duration and which gives the maximum amount of traction with the minimum amount of discomfort to the patient's chin and jaw.

Cervical traction techniques can also be applied to patients who are not hospitalized. Home traction apparatus can be purchased at any surgical supply house and in some drug stores, but this type of equipment cannot be used for applying intermittent traction, which has been shown to give the best results.

METHOD OF APPLICATION

The patient is given hot packs and massage before traction is applied.

The patient is usually placed in a sitting position with the head and neck flexed (bent forward).

Traction is applied, starting with 10 pounds.

The traction is held for 2 seconds, and then the patient rests for 3 seconds.

Total treatment time is usually 15 minutes.

The weight is gradually increased by 2 pounds at each treatment until the total weight is 20 to 30 pounds, if the patient can tolerate the increase.

While hospitalized, the patient receives traction daily. Outpatients receive therapy three times a week for a series of at least 10 to 15 treatments.

11
EXERCISE

Therapeutic exercise is bodily movement prescribed to restore normal function or to maintain a state of well-being. The exercise program for each patient is developed according to his needs and is based on medical evaluation of his disability; however, the purpose of all exercise is to restore, improve, or maintain one or more of the following:

Strength (power), i.e., the ability of the muscle to contract
Stretch (elasticity), i.e., the ability of the muscle to give up contraction and yield to passive stretch
Coordination, i.e., the ability of the muscle to work with other muscles in proper timing and with appropriate strength and elasticity

TYPES OF MUSCLE CONTRACTION

Muscle contraction is described according to the changes it produces in the muscle's length and tension:

Isometric contraction — the length of the muscle remains unchanged; no movement is produced (only holding power); tension is increased.
Isotonic contraction — the length of the muscle decreases or increases; movement is produced; tension remains unchanged.
Concentric contraction — the muscle becomes shorter; tension may increase or remain unchanged.
Eccentric contraction — the muscle becomes longer; tension is generally unchanged but may increase if resistance is applied.

TYPES OF MOVEMENT EMPLOYED
IN THERAPEUTIC EXERCISES

Passive — movements are performed by someone other than the patient; no muscle action occurs and the patient exerts no effort. Passive movement should be administered with great care. A muscle spasm is a danger signal; if it occurs, the movement should be stopped. Tightening of a muscle precedes pain; to secure best results, all movements should be well below the limit at which pain occurs. One movement through its fullest range is much better than a series of movements through a shorter range. The chief aim of passive exercise is to prevent contractures and the formation of definite adhesions. Passive movements are frequently employed in the gentlest possible form in early mobilization of joints following fractures.

Active — movements are performed by the patient, who voluntarily contracts and relaxes the muscles that control a particular movement. The patient makes the entire effort at motion himself, without assistance from the therapist. All postural exercises are in this category, as well as exercises for flatfoot, scoliosis, lordosis, kyphosis, and abdominal exercises. Active exercises are also employed for the correction of certain muscular and circulatory disturbances such as occur in poliomyelitis, cerebral palsy, cardiac deficiency, and peripheral vascular disease, and to hasten restoration of function following trauma.

One form of active exercise is muscle setting, in which a muscle or group of muscles is actively contracted and relaxed without producing motion of the joint that it ordinarily mobilizes. This exercise may be employed while an extremity is in a cast — quadriceps setting to prevent atrophy, for example.

Assistive — the patient is helped to perform the movement. The therapist, or some mechanical agent, assists the patient to extend the motion still farther. This type of exercise is employed chiefly in mobilization of joints around which there are slight contractures. Usually heat and massage are given to relax the part before doing these exercises. If fibrillation of muscles occurs, the muscles have been given too great a task and assistance is needed. The operator should increase the range of movement daily to enable the patient to gradually shift from assistive to active exercises.

Resistive — the patient performs movement against resistance. This may be provided by the therapist, or the patient may use some of his own antagonistic groups of muscles to produce resistance, or weights and other apparatus may provide resistance that may be measured accurately. In general, active resistive exercises are used for strengthening muscles.

Orders for these exercises should specify the length of time for the exercises to continue, the weights to be lifted, and the resistance to be applied. The time and energy used should be increased gradually.

TYPES OF THERAPEUTIC EXERCISES

Range of motion (ROM) — movement of the joint through its full range in all appropriate planes; may be passive, active, or resistive

Muscle reeducation — exercises to help a muscle or muscle group "relearn" its normal function; used chiefly in cases of weakness and/or loss of coordination following disuse, paralysis, or surgical procedures

Pressive resistance exercises (PRE) — exercises to increase resistance (performed manually or with apparatus) in order to strengthen a muscle, muscle group, or supportive structures surrounding a joint

Endurance — low-resistance, high-repetition exercises to increase muscle endurance

Coordination — exercises designed to improve precision of muscle movements, i.e., use of the proper muscle at the proper time with the exact amount of force necessary

Relaxation — exercises to promote release of prolonged muscular contractions; the patient is taught to be aware of muscular tensions and how to control and inhibit them

Postural — exercises designed to maintain a proper relationship between the body parts

Conditioning — exercises designed to maintain and/or strengthen some or all of the body musculature

Stretching — exercises to restore normal range of motion using active and/or passive measures when loss of elasticity of soft tissue has resulted in joint limitation

Breathing — exercises and breathing practices used to correct and minimize respiratory deficits or to improve trunk and postural stability

PHYSIOLOGICAL EFFECTS OF EXERCISE

Exercise may increase cardiac output as much as four or five times its base level. It may increase the blood flow through active muscles as much as 20 times the flow during rest. Both arterial and venous blood pressures are elevated during exercise. There is an immediate rise in the respiratory rate with the initiation of exercise and general body metabolism is stimulated. Muscular activity results in diminution of urinary output; following exercise the urine may be concentrated, and there may be transitory increases in its content of albumin, sugar, nitrogen, and chlorides.

CONDITIONS THAT CAN BE HELPED
BY VARIOUS TYPES OF EXERCISE

Among the most important common conditions that physicians see in their practice, and exercises that may be helpful in relieving them, include the following:

Weakened Abdominal Muscles

Supine Position

1. Raise feet, first singly, then together (knees extended), just 10 inches from the floor.
2. Flatten the lower back against the floor, thus rotating the pelvis backward by contracting the abdominal muscles.
3. With knees flexed and heels close to hips, lift hips and hold.
4. From position as in 3, bring the flexed knees slowly

over the chest and close to face. This stretches the lower back muscles without bringing the psoas into use. Very useful in lordosis.

5. In the same position as 3 and 4, alternately bend and straighten the knees as in bicycle riding. Keep hips off the floor.

6. In the same position again, bring each knee alternately to the opposite shoulder. This strengthens the internal and external oblique muscles.

Sitting Position

1. With hands on hips, twist the body alternately to the right and left; repeat with hands on neck, arms shoulder high; repeat with arms overhead.

2. With hands on hips, fix the pelvis and circumduct the trunk by bending the body forward, to the left, backwards, and to the right, forward again and up. Repeat in opposite direction.

Standing Position

1. Trunk flexion — bend the trunk alternately to the right and left without twisting, with hands first on hips, then on neck, and finally with arms raised sidewise shoulder high. Avoid swaying the hips forward.

2. Trunk torsion — fix the hips firmly, using body above the hips only; with hands on hips, turn the trunk on its long axis alternately to the right and left.

3. Trunk circling — with feet slightly apart, hands behind neck, fix the hips and circumduct the trunk, first bending forward, to the right, backward and to the left. Then again forward and up. Repeat in the opposite direction.

Arthritis   see pages 94–106

Bell's Palsy   see pages 140–142

Bursitis

1. Use the shoulder wheel.
2. Swing the arms anteroposteriorly and mediolaterally from a stooped position.
3. Place the hand of the affected arm on the opposite shoulder posteriorly.
4. Touch the floor with the hands without bending the knees.
5. Hold the arm out horizontally so that the fingers just touch the wall, then attempt to "climb the wall" with the fingers of the abducted arm.

Flatfoot

Exercises are a most important factor in the treatment of flatfoot. Active and resistive exercises should be carried out twice daily in bare or stockinged feet.

1. Stand barefoot with the feet parallel and about 2 inches apart, straddling a seam in a rug. On the count of one, force the feet apart without actually allowing them to move apart, thus throwing the weight on their outer borders; on the count of two, allow them to roll in slowly but not all the way. Repeat this 10 times at first, with a gradual daily increase to as many as 100 times.
2. Same as 1, but hold the big toes together and on the floor.
3. Straddle a seam in a rug or a line on the floor and walk across the room with all the weight on the outer borders of the feet and toes curled downward and inward. Make the round trip five times.
4. Same as 3, but raise each foot so that it is opposite the other knee and walk across the room using the so-called "ostrich step." Weight must at all times be borne on the outer border of the foot.
5. Hold the feet parallel and maintain the knees in a straight position. Roll knees outward, which

automatically causes the longitudinal arches to rise. Repeat from 10 to 25 times.

6. Rise on toes, tilt the weight to the outer borders, and come down in two counts. Repeat from 10 to 25 times.
7. Use a supination board about 6 inches high and 8 feet long, its sloping sides being at the angle of an equilateral triangle. Walk the length of the board three to four times as one would walk on the ridge of a housetop.

Hemiplegia   see pages 143–149

Injuries

After certain types of injuries, whether fracture, dislocation, sprain, or strain, in which a particular extremity or part has been immobilized, a certain amount of stiffness and limitation of motion results. This necessitates certain movements in order to return that part to normal function. There should be a gradual transition of movements from muscle setting to active movements. Active movements are always the treatment of choice.

Limited Movement of Foot and Ankle

1. Rotate foot, right foot clockwise, left foot counter-clockwise.
2. Pick up marbles with toes.
3. Gather towel under foot and toes.
4. Pull up arches; roll foot to outside with toes down.
5. Rise up on toes; shift weight to outside of foot.
6. Stand between two chairs with the affected foot 12 inches in front of the other foot. Rock to and fro in this position, keeping affected foot flat on the floor.

Limited Extension of Knee

1. Do knee cap setup or quadriceps setting.
2. Straighten leg, using resistance.

3. Sit on floor or in bed with knees as straight as possible. Place hands on knees and press them downward by swinging forward with upper part of back and shoulder, keeping elbows straight.
4. Stand, bend forward, and place hands on the knees. Keep elbows straight and force knees backward by swinging the shoulders and upper part of back downward.

Limited Flexion of Knee

1. Do muscle setting or knee cap setup.
2. Lie on abdomen. Make a complete turn of a bandage around the foot and ankle. Grasp both ends of bandage and attempt to flex the knee by pulling up on the bandage.
3. From a position on the hands and knees, sit backward on the heels.
4. Standing, grasp the back of a chair with the hands. Bend the knees and assume a squatting position, placing the weight of the body on the toes.
5. Bend and straighten the leg.
6. Bicycle while in supine position.
7. Do quarter- and half-knee bend.
8. Climb stairs.

Limited Neck Movement

1. Move head forward and backward.
2. Move head to side, right and left.
3. Rotate head.
4. Roll head against towel resistance.
5. Move head backward against hand resistance.
6. Lying on back, with weight on back of head, roll from side to side.
7. Lying face down, with weight on forehead, roll from side to side.

Limited Shoulder Movement

1. Raise the arms sideward shoulder high. Swing the arms upward and backward in a circular motion, gradually increasing the size of the circles.
2. Shrug the shoulders in upward and downward and circular motion.
3. Creep up a wall with the fingers, reaching higher each day, with the arm extended directly in front of the body, then with the arm extended laterally.
4. Lie on the abdomen with hands at back of neck and raise both elbows and head.
5. Use parallel bars.
6. Do push-up, leaning.
7. Do push-up, kneeling.
8. Use shoulder wheel.
9. Use wall weight.
10. Use internal rotator.
11. Use shoulder roller.

Limited Elbow Movement

1. Bend and straighten elbow.
2. Pull wall weights.
3. Bend against force.
4. Straighten against force.
5. Do doorknob-turning exercise.
6. Use shoulder wheel.
7. Do push-ups.
8. Do wall push.

Limited Wrist Movement

1. Rest the forearm firmly on a table with the wrist extending over the edge. Bend wrist upward, then downward, as far as possible.
2. Extend arms forward with the palms of the hands together. Bring the forearms back to the chest by bending the elbows. Keep palms together.

Limited Finger Movement

1. Rest the entire hand flat on a table. Spread fingers and thumb widely apart, then bring them together again.
2. Make an O by touching the thumb to each fingertip in turn.
3. Squeeze a small rubber ball or sponge held in the palm of the hand.

Limited Hip Movement

1. Stand between two chairs. Swing the affected thigh backward and forward.
2. Lie on back, clasp the bent knee with both arms, and force the knee against chest.
3. Sit with feet spread 12 inches apart and roll the foot and leg inward and outward.
4. Lie on back. Raise lower leg slowly, first with the knee bent and then with the knee straight.
5. Lie on back with knees straight. Slide legs wide apart and then return to starting position.
6. Stand beside a table. Rest buttock and leg of the normal side along the edge of the table, allowing the affected leg to swing free. Swing the affected leg back and forth from hip.
7. Lie on abdomen and extend thigh backward, keeping knees straight.
8. Do trunk-twister exercise.
9. Do pelvic-twister exercise.
10. Do pelvic-roller exercise.

Metatarsal Arch Disturbances (Fallen Arches)

The following exercises have been found to be of great benefit in increasing the power of the supporting structures and the flexibility of the metatarsal arch. Each exercise is done with bare feet twice daily.

Doorstop Exercise

Two old-fashioned doorstops, obtainable at hardware stores, are prepared for use by removal of the rubber tips. They are then screwed onto a board about 14 inches long, 8 inches wide, and 2 inches thick. The centers of the doorstops should be 6 inches apart.

The board is placed on the floor and the patient sits on a chair in front of it. Each foot is placed on a doorstop with very slight pressure just behind the metatarsal bones. On the count of one the toes are forcibly curled down, and on the count of two they are allowed to relax slowly. This is continued until a count of 200 has been reached.

Towel Exercise

The patient sits in a chair. A large hand towel is spread on the carpet with the narrow edge facing the patient. The feet are placed so that half of each foot is on the towel. The towel is grasped first with the toes of one foot, then with the toes of the other. As the toes of one foot grasp, those of the other relax. This is continued until the entire towel is under the feet.

Golf-ball Exercise

A golf ball is placed on the rug and rolled under the metatarsal arch for one minute. Then it is picked up with the toes of one foot and placed under the toes of the other foot and the exercise repeated for one minute. The patient repeats the maneuver six times.

Marble Exercise

Marbles of various sizes are placed on a rug. The patient sits in a chair and picks up marbles with his toes.

Pencil Exercise

A round pencil is placed on a hard floor, and by means of curled-down toes, the patient pushes and pulls the pencil around the floor with short, quick movements.

Shortened Heel Tendon

1. Walk on the heels across the room five times.
2. Do a quarter knee bend with the heels flat.
3. Place ball of foot on block; weight pushes the heel down.
4. Lean toward wall, body straight, heels on floor.

CONTRAINDICATIONS FOR EXERCISE

Exercise and motion of the various portions of the body are normal procedures. The danger is that specified exercises may be overdone or performed incorrectly. For instance, if exercise following a fracture is too vigorous, applied too early, or administered without proper support, union may be disrupted and the bone refractured.

Excessive or too early exercise of a joint following injury may produce further trauma and may result in ankylosis.

Excessive exercise may lead to cardiac strain in the young person or to acute dilatation of the heart with fatal results in an older individual.

In the presence of cardiac disease, exercise must always be employed with caution.

III

CONDITIONS
COMMONLY TREATED
BY PHYSICAL THERAPY

12
AMPUTATION

The person who has had a limb amputated is usually referred to an orthopedic consultant following the surgery. However, there are many physical therapy modalities that may be used before the patient is ready for his prosthesis, and the general practitioner is often the one who will treat the amputee during this period and who will decide on the modalities to be used.

TREATMENT

The main objective of physical therapy for the amputee is to prepare the stump for early and efficient use of a prosthesis. Modalities used are heat, massage, and exercise. Whirlpool baths are the preferred source of heat; they improve circulation and relieve pain caused by persistent edema or excessive formation of periosteal connective tissue. Massage is given later on when there is no infection. Early exercise of the remaining part of the limb results in reduction of edema and is good preparation for the use of an artificial limb. Contrast baths are helpful in increasing circulation.

13
BURNS

One of the most serious complications of burns is the development of deformities caused by the contraction of scar tissue. During the healing of burns that have destroyed the entire thickness of the skin, fibrous tissue must necessarily form to compensate for the loss occasioned by the burn. Once formed, this meshwork of interlacing collagen fibers undergoes a period of active contraction, and the forces exerted in this vital process are considerable. The value of physical therapy in the treatment of burns is that it minimizes the process of fibrosis.

The degree of scarring that develops following a burn depends to a large extent upon the efficacy of the treatment and medication, and on the healing reactions of the patient.

Treatment should be instituted as soon as possible after the injury. Everything is to be gained by avoiding contractures, because, once formed, their correction is difficult and time consuming.

TREATMENT

The following modalities have proved useful in the treatment of burns:

1. *Massage* stimulates the blood supply to the burned area, helps to reduce the amount of scar tissue that develops, loosens scars and overcomes a tendency for them to retract or contract, and helps to restore function of the involved joints.
2. *Dry heat* from various sources relieves pain.
3. *Hydrotherapy,* in the form of whirlpool baths, Hubbard tub baths, paraffin baths, and contrast baths, helps to increase movement and motion.

4. *Dry cold* overcomes traumatic and postoperative swelling.
5. *Ultraviolet irradiation* improves the patient's general condition, stimulates healing, overcomes low-grade infections, and prepares the burned area for plastic surgery.

14
DERMATOLOGIC CONDITIONS

The general practitioner frequently uses certain physical therapy modalities in treating common skin disorders before he refers the patient to a dermatologist. Ultraviolet radiation is one such modality. The physician who prescribes these rays and the therapist who administers them must remember that diseased or inflamed skin and skin with eruptions is more resistant to ultraviolet radiation and can tolerate much heavier dosages than normal skin. Consequently, normal skin surrounding an area to be treated must be protected either by a suitable covering or a sunburn preventative. It is also desirable to remove any exudate and to cleanse the skin of grease, oil, and medications with alcohol, ether, or acetone before administering ultraviolet radiation.

ACNE VULGARIS

Acne vulgaris may be treated with ultraviolet irradiation two or three times a week, in doses sufficient to produce mild erythema; exposure need not be so intense as to produce blistering. In many cases, especially when the comedones are numerous, ultraviolet radiation produced by a cold quartz lamp gives a better response. When acne vulgaris is extensive, it may be necessary to administer suberythemal doses of ultraviolet rays to the entire body as well as more intensive doses to the affected areas. The patient should be informed that deep acne lesions will probably result in prominent scars or pits and that this disfigurement is due to the nature of the disease, not the treatment.

ALOPECIA AREATA

Before irradiation with ultraviolet light, the bald spot is painted with phenol, which is later removed with alcohol. This treatment should be given twice weekly in sufficient dosage to produce erythema but no blisters.

BOILS AND CARBUNCLES

Ultraviolet radiation can be used in the treatment of boils and carbuncles, provided the dosage prescribed is three to four times the minimal erythemal dose. If the size of the discharging area permits, the area should be covered between treatments with a material that will exclude the air, such as Elastoplast. When started very early, this treatment is quite helpful.

ECZEMA SEBORRHEICUM

Ultraviolet irradiation appears to give good results in eczema, especially when erythemal doses are used for the chronic dry patches. For the nonexuding generalized type of dermatitis seborrheica, suberythemal doses given daily to the entire body are beneficial. The best results are obtained when appropriate topical remedies, systemic treatment, and ultraviolet radiation are used simultaneously.

LUPUS VULGARIS

Ultraviolet radiation is used in doses sufficient to cause third-degree erythema. The treatment is repeated after the erythema has subsided. The course of treatment for lupus vulgaris may last for many months.

NEURODERMATITIS

General ultraviolet irradiation of the body is of value in neurodermatitis. Cabinet baths and sauna baths are also beneficial.

PSORIASIS

Exposure to ultraviolet rays (mild erythemal dose) is one of the modalities used for the treatment of psoriasis during the nonacute stage. The most practical method of treating extensive psoriasis is by exposing the entire body to natural sunlight daily. One authority recommends application of 2 to 3% coal tar ointment to all lesions, the night before the body is irradiated. In the morning the excess ointment is wiped off with oil before the patient is exposed to ultraviolet light.

SCAR TISSUE

Scarring may involve the skin only, or it may extend into deeper tissues surrounding joints, tendons, and nerves. Forceful manipulation of scar tissue only results in tearing and further scarring.

Treatment consists of the application of hot moist packs, ultrasonic therapy, friction type of massage, and active exercise and stretching. Severe scarring may require surgical treatment.

SCLERODERMA

Scleroderma is a chronic localized or diffused skin disease of unknown etiology characterized by fibrosis, rigidity, and atrophy of the skin and subcutaneous tissue. In addition to whatever medication the physician may prescribe, iontophoresis with a 1% solution of Mecholyl chloride is most helpful as an adjunct in treatment.

ULCERS AND INFECTED WOUNDS

Ultraviolet radiation is the modality usually employed to help clear up the sepsis caused by infected wounds and ulcers. It stimulates regeneration of epithelium and, in chronic ulcers, improves defective circulation and poor nutrition.

The therapist carefully cleanses the surface of the ulcer of any discharge and all traces of ointment, and it is advisable to use a heat lamp to heat the area to be treated for 30 minutes. Then ultraviolet irradiation of sufficient dosage to produce second degree erythema is applied, with the source at a distance of about 18 inches from the area to be treated. A mild antiseptic ointment, or one prescribed by the physician, is applied after the treatment. Irradiation is repeated at two- to three-day intervals. When the ulcer appears to be cleaner and granulation begins to take place, only first-degree or suberythemal doses of irradiation should be employed.

For sluggish ulcers, ultraviolet irradiation of sufficient dosage to cause a first- or second-degree erythema as a stimulation is worth trying. Treatment should be given three times a week.

For treating chronic leg ulcers in patients with poor circulation, use of the whirlpool bath at a temperature of 105°F for 25 to 30 minutes will cleanse the ulcer and improve the circulation; this should be followed by ultraviolet irradiation.

Widespread simple ulcers or multiple varicose ulcers respond well to Mecholyl iontophoresis.

15
EYE, EAR, NOSE, AND THROAT CONDITIONS

Many of the common eye, ear, nose, and throat conditions may be treated by the general practitioner and are helped by common modalities found in the physician's office or in the home. Although some of the treatments used may be old-fashioned, they are helpful in many conditions.

EYE

Conjunctivitis, Acute

For the first 24 hours, cold compresses should be applied; then moist or dry heat.

Meibomitis, Chronic

Massage of the lids is very helpful.

EAR

Eczema of the Auricle

Ultraviolet irradiation is helpful and worth a trial.

Otitis Externa

Heat should be applied in the form of hot wet compresses of either magnesium sulfate, boric acid, or aluminum acetate. After drainage is established, some form of heat may again be used.

Otitis Media, Chronic

Ultraviolet irradiation and short wave diathermy (air-spaced application technique) may be used. Some physicians recommend zinc iontophoresis by a special technique; it too is worth a trial.

NOSE

Nasal Furunculosis

Hot wet compresses, which may or may not be saturated with magnesium sulfate or boric acid solution, are of value. Infrared radiation affords a convenient and effective form of heat, too. Infrared should be applied at a distance of about 18 inches for a duration of 20 minutes, every 3 to 4 hours. This treatment will relieve pain and encourage localization of the infection.

Sinusitis

Hot, moist Turkish towels should be applied over the sinuses, with an infrared lamp directed at the towels. Diathermy may be used if there is drainage, and should be applied at low intensity for about 20 to 25 minutes with the air-spaced technique or a special sinus applicator.

THROAT

Laryngitis

In the acute stage heat may be helpful. Heat treatment may be given in the form of infrared irradiation, hot compresses, or diathermy with electrodes placed on each side of the neck. Inhalation of steam with various medications is also very helpful. Cold compresses are sometimes used.

Pharyngitis

Infrared heat, diathermy, and hot compresses are useful Ultraviolet irradiation may also be used in the region of the inflamed pharynx.

Tonsillitis

Hot compresses, infrared heat to the neck, and short-wave diathermy, with the electrodes placed on either side of the neck, may be used.

16
GENITOURINARY DISORDERS

Many urinary tract infections can be helped by early use of physical therapy, often before drug therapy can relieve the symptoms. A patient complaining of a genitourinary lesion or disease will often see his family physician before he is referred to a urologist; the general practitioner can frequently relieve the acute symptoms by prescribing various types of physical therapy in conjunction with drug medication. Such modalities as diathermy, infrared and radiant heat, and various low voltage currents may be used.

PROSTATIC DISORDERS

For acute inflammation, local heating by diathermy, hot irrigations, or hot sitz baths are very helpful in conjunction with drug medication or any other form of treatment that may be prescribed.

CYSTITIS

The pain and spasm associated with the onset of acute cystitis can be greatly relieved by heat-producing methods, such as hot sitz baths, hot packs to the suprapubic area, infrared radiation to the suprapubic and perineal regions, and diathermy applied by a special electrode. Physical therapy is especially helpful before the symptoms are relieved by antibiotics, but it may be continued throughout the entire period of infection.

KIDNEY DISORDERS

Heat applied locally to the renal area, by means of warm baths, hot packs, hot-water bottles, infrared lamps, or diathermy, may give an effective measure of relief from pain of kidney origin, both the colic of acute obstruction and the dull ache associated with other renal conditions. Mild massage is helpful in relieving painful muscle spasm. Diathermy may be used also as an adjunct to other methods in the treatment of oliguria or anuria resulting from crystallization of sulfa drugs within the tubules. Ultraviolet radiation, local and general, is still used — along with chemotherapy — by some urologists in the treatment of sinuses following nephrectomy for renal tuberculosis.

SPASM OF URETER

Local application of infrared heat or diathermy may be of great help in producing relaxation of the ureter when spasm due to a calculus or trauma from instrumental examination of the ureter is present.

17
MUSCULOSKELETAL DISORDERS

Many physical therapy modalities are beneficial in treating common musculoskeletal disorders. The physician's evaluation of the patient's pain, its type, location, and severity can be helpful in diagnosing the difficulty and in deciding on the therapy to be employed.

FACTORS IN THE EVALUATION OF PAIN

1. Pain that occurs after rest and improves with movement is often a sign of osteoarthritic joints and of mild sprains and strains.
2. Pain that occurs upon weight bearing is often a sign of "static" deficiency or overstrain of the lower extremities.
3. Pain that occurs on movement of a joint and ceases when the joint is at rest is often a sign of acute joint condition or injury, or of sprain or strain.
4. Pain that occurs while one is working, or after work, may indicate an occupational source.
5. Pain that occurs immediately after injury may denote a fracture or major tear of muscle, ligament, or tissue.
6. Pain that occurs after an interval is most often the consequence of minor strain or sprain.
7. Pain that radiates along the distribution of a nerve may suggest radiculitis or mechanical interference; for example, lesions of the nucleus pulposus or impingement on the nerve by contracted muscles.

ARTHRITIS AND RHEUMATIC CONDITIONS

Treatment

Because of the many physical therapy modalities available to the physician, he is sometimes at a loss to determine which to prescribe for patients with arthritis or a rheumatic condition. In general, he may employ the following plan:

1. Moist heat or very mild infrared radiation is applied for about 30 minutes two to three times daily, for acutely or subacutely inflamed joints.

2. No massage or exercise is given during the acute stage of arthritis, except that the involved joint is moved through a full range of painless (or nearly painless) motion two to three times each day to minimize the formation of dense adhesions.

3. In subacute and chronic stages, the triad of heat, massage, and graded exercises is used daily for practically every patient. The form of heat at this stage should be that which is most comfortable to the patient and at the same time produces the best results. Moist heat, infrared lamps, baking, warm paraffin applications, warm tub baths, diathermy, etc., may be tried, and whichever seems to suit the particular patient should be continued.

4. In subacute and chronic stages, physical therapy is administered at least once daily, preferably more often, regardless of whether the patient is at the hospital or at home. If he is at home, daily home therapeutic measures are supplemented, in most cases, by treatments at a hospital or physical therapy clinic or by a physician.

Therapy must not be confined to two or three treatments per week at the physician's office. The doctor must take time to explain the role of therapy in the home to the patient and his family.

Heat

In the acute stage, heat should not be used in any form, including diathermy and hot baths. Efforts should be made to keep the patient comfortable by rest, use of splints, and medication. In nonacute stages, various forms of heat may be used.

Infrared radiation. This is probably the most convenient form of heat to use. An infrared lamp or a coil with a reflector may be used, or even an ordinary household electric heater. These appliances should be kept 18 inches from the part being treated. Treatments may last from 30 to 45 minutes, and be given two to three times daily.

Homemade bakers. An electrician in the community can assemble such an outfit (see page 13). The treated area should be covered with a towel or sheet and the baker used for 30 minutes. The treatment may be repeated two to three times daily and followed by massage if the arthritis is not acute.

Electric heating pads. The patient may use an electric heating pad at a low heat provided the part treated is wrapped in a towel to prevent burns; the treatment may be used two to three times daily for 45 minutes.

Diathermy and microwave diathermy. Treatments can be given in the doctor's office or in a clinic and should be administered by an experienced technician or by the physician. Directions for use and length of treatments are up to the person in charge of the individual patient. Important suggestions and contraindications for diathermy will be found in the section on diathermy (see pages 7–20).

Paraffin baths. Useful particularly in treating hands and fingers (see page 59 for method).

Hot tub baths. These should be taken daily before the exercises. The temperature of the water should not exceed 102°F. Localized hot tub baths for hand, forearm, and foot may be taken in water up to 108°F. No hot tub bath, either localized or generalized, should last longer than 20 minutes.

Hot fomentations (for areas such as shoulders, elbows, and knees). Fold a piece of woolen blanket, flannel, or a

Turkish towel and dip it in hot water (115°F). Wring it out, apply to the area to be treated, and cover it immediately with another towel or blanket to keep the heat in. Repeat the procedure as often as necessary for 20 minutes. Flaxseed or oatmeal poultices are equally effective.

Contrast baths. These are particularly beneficial for the hands and feet, and may be done twice daily (for method, see pages 51–52).

Massage

Massage should be started as soon as the acute inflammatory process in the joint has subsided, as judged by diminished redness, swelling, and tenderness. Massage may be given within several weeks after the onset of acute arthritis requiring bed rest. At the onset only the tissues surrounding the joints should be massaged lightly to promote absorption of the periarticular edema. If the knees are involved, the muscles of the thighs and lower legs are massaged to aid the return of venous blood and to prevent muscular atrophy from disuse. In chronic arthritis, the surrounding muscles and areas over the joints themselves may be included if the massage is given very lightly.

Massage should be preceded by some form of heat and should begin with gentle stroking, to be followed later by deeper stroking motions, kneading, and friction of the surrounding muscles; superficial stroking (very light) may be started over the joint. Massage should never cause pain. It is better to give too little than too much. Unless contraindicated, every patient with nonacute rheumatoid arthritis should have this treatment for 10 to 15 minutes twice a day.

Massage is contraindicated when the following conditions are present:

1. Acute inflamed joints
2. Fever
3. Increased pain, swelling, or stiffness in joint persisting more than two hours following massage
4. Suspicion of local malignancy
5. Phlebitis or lymphangitis
6. Suspicion of osteomyelitis or tuberculosis of bone

Range of Motion Exercises

Too often a patient feels that if he is working he is getting all the exercise he needs. In many cases, this is not necessarily the type of exercise he should have. An affected joint should be carried through its full range of motion several times each day (see Figure 2). This does not happen in the course of one's ordinary daily occupation. If exercises are carefully carried out in bed, without the strain of weight bearing, they are more easily done.

The purposes of the exercises are, first, to strengthen muscles that are needed to maintain good bone position within a joint, and, second, to increase joint motion. This will be accomplished only by putting a joint through its full range of motion up to the tolerance of pain, at least a few times each day.

All types of exercise have a place in the therapy of arthritis, ranging from passive exercise to active assistive, to active, to active resistive (see page 67–68). If a joint is exercised too much, the arthritis is aggravated; if it is moved too little, however, motion becomes limited. To guide the patient between these two extremes, the following rules should be observed:

1. Any exercise that produces pain during the same or the following day should be reduced in frequency or stopped.
2. Any exercise that is painful only at the time, or for an hour or two afterwards, is beneficial.

Even in the most acute cases of rheumatoid arthritis, a patient can do a few muscle setting exercises before he becomes tired. Exercises done two or three times can be repeated several times a day, and in a day or two, the number of exercises can be increased by one or two. The patient should have at least two exercise periods a day, and as his tolerance increases, exercise periods can be increased to five to ten times a day. Instructions for specific joint exercises follow:

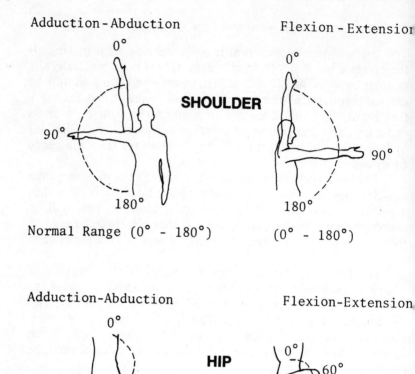

Adduction - Abduction

0°

SHOULDER

90°

180°

Normal Range (0° - 180°)

Flexion - Extension

0°

90°

180°

(0° - 180°)

Adduction-Abduction

0°

HIP

150°

180°

Normal Range (180°-150°)

Flexion-Extension

0°

60°

180°

(180°-60°)

Figure 2. Range of motion chart for shoulder, hip, elbow, knee, and ankle joints. (Reproduced from pp. 12–13, chap. 20, vol. 1 of *Practice of Medicine,* by permission of the Medical Department, Harper & Row, Publishers, Inc., Hagerstown, Maryland.)

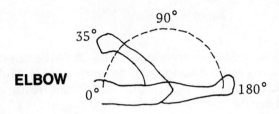

ELBOW

Flexion-Extension   Normal Range (35°-180°)

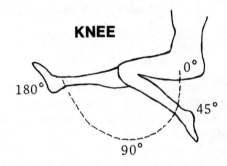

KNEE

Flexion-Extension   Normal Range (45°-180°)

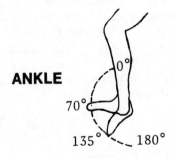

ANKLE

Dorsal-Planter Flexion   Normal Range (70°-135°)

99

Hand and wrist

1. Make a fist.
2. Stretch the fingers as straight as possible. If the fingers remain bent, rest the hand palm down on a table. Hold the other hand firmly on top of it and raise forearm of affected arm in an effort to flatten bent fingers.
3. Spread fingers apart.
4. Touch the tip of each finger to the end of the thumb, making as round a circle as possible.
5. Bend wrist forward and backward as far as possible.
6. Move fingers toward thumb.
7. Turn wrist slowly back and forth as though turning a doorknob.

Elbow

1. Lying on the back, with the upper arm resting on the bed, bring fingers to the top of the shoulder.
2. With palm turned up, bring hand down to the bed while straightening elbow.

Shoulder

1. Standing with arms resting at sides, palms toward the body, raise the arm sideways as far as possible away from the body, then return; then raise the arm forward, upward, and as far back as it will go, then return.
2. Lying on the back with legs straight and arm at sides, raise the arm forward, upward, and back as far as it will go, then swing the arm out to the side and around the back to side of body.

Ankle

1. Bend foot up and down slowly.
2. Alternately turn foot in and out slowly.
3. Sitting on the edge of the bed, move the foot through a circular motion.

Knee

1. Lying on the back with the leg straight, contract the muscles of the entire leg, tightening the knee cap and flattening the knee down on the bed.
2. Sitting on a rigid bed or table with the legs hanging over the edge and above the floor, slowly straighten legs and lower again, alternately.
3. Sitting on the bed with legs straight, raise the knee off the bed, sliding the foot back and thus bending and straightening the leg alternately.
4. Lying on the back, ride bicycle.

Hip

1. Lying on the back, hold the legs straight and move them 15 inches to the side and then back.
2. Lying on the back, raise and lower legs slowly, with the knees first straight and then bent.
3. Lying face down, move the leg backward, keeping the knee straight.

Stretching Exercises

People with poor posture develop shortened muscles and tendons. If arthritis develops in such a person, it becomes doubly important to stretch these shortened structures. Instructions for stretching exercises follow:

1. Lying on the back with legs straight, flatten the neck against the bed by making a double chin and at the same time stretch up through the top of the head, making yourself as tall as possible.
2. Sit with legs straight out and bend forward, attempting to touch the toes with the fingertips without bending the knees. This exercises the muscles of the back of the legs; it is also good for maintaining motion in the hip.
3. Lying on the back with knees bent and feet on the bed, raise one knee toward the chest; straighten knee by

lifting foot in the air and stretching up with the heel; let the knee bend and the foot return to the starting position.

4. Lying on the back with legs straight, turn the cheek as far as possible toward the bed; then stretch the head up, keeping the shoulders flat on the bed. Come back to straight position and rest. Repeat, turning the head to the other side.

5. By using a sling which works over a pulley attached to the head of the bed or hung from a door, it is possible to stretch the neck muscles and counteract a tendency to abnormal curvature. The physician should be able to guide a carpenter or handyman in making such a sling. This type of sling is also a very satisfactory form of treatment for chronic neck and shoulder pain, so common among arthritic patients.

Postural Exercises for Ambulatory Patients

Lying on the back with legs straight, tighten buttock muscles and retract or pull in the abdominal muscles, flattening the abdomen. Do not hold the breath. Make an effort to get the lower back flat against the bed, thus straightening out the curve of the lower back. This position represents the starting point for the following basic postural exercises:

1. Clasp hands in back of the neck and slowly bend one knee, sliding the foot back, then the other. Hold the back flat and slowly slide the feet out until legs are extended.

2. With arms crossed on the chest, tighten buttock muscles and retract abdomen. Raise head and shoulders 6 to 8 inches from bed.

3. With hands at the sides, tighten buttock muscles and retract abdomen. Raise arms over head and inhale. Keep back flat. Lower arms and exhale.

4. With arms at the sides, tighten buttock muscles and retract abdomen. Roll the arms outward, turning palms upward, and force the shoulders back. Keep the lower

back against the bed. Try to press the back of the neck against bed, keeping the chin in.
5. With hands in back of the neck, tighten buttock muscles and retract abdomen. Slowly raise and lower alternate leg, keeping the knees straight.

Other postural exercises include:

1. Standing with the back against the wall, heels 3 inches from wall, feet 3 inches apart, put the hands in the back of the neck, bend knees, tighten buttock muscles and retract abdomen. Hold back flat against wall and straighten knees.
2. Lying face down, with a pillow under the abdomen, legs straight, tighten buttock muscles and retract abdomen.
3. Lying face down with a pillow under the abdomen, arms shoulder-high and elbow bent to a right angle, tighten buttock muscles and retract abdomen. Raise arms and hands from the bed, bringing the shoulder blades together.

Resting Joints

Bed rest. For most efficient rest, the joint should be kept as straight as possible. Arthritic patients must avoid developing flexed or bent joints. They must remember that lying in bed with fingers, wrists, elbows, and knees bent, although it may seem temporarily more comfortable, leads to further disability. When the patient is lying on his back, a small sandbag or folded towel placed under the upper arm and another at the wrist will help keep the elbow and wrist straight. The hands should be turned with the palms upward. It is possible to design a light plaster or aluminum gutter splint to hold fingers and hands straight, which the patient can wear at intervals during the day and at night. A folded towel placed under the ankle will help straighten the knee when the patient is lying on his back. Pillows should not be placed under the knees in any case. A small pillow may sometimes be used under the head.

Footboards and sandbags can help to keep the feet in good position. Feet generally tend to turn out when one is supine; this strains the knee. Sandbags placed against the outside of the feet remove such strain. The weight of the bedcovers also tends to turn the feet outward. A board 3 or 4 inches wide, placed on edge across the foot of the bed under the covers, will take their weight off the feet.

Bedboards are a good remedy for beds that are too soft. When a patient lies on a soft bed his spine takes on the curves of the mattress, and he wakens unrested and often with back pain. A bedboard made of one-inch plywood, running the full length and width of the bed and placed between the mattress and spring, will give proper support and maintain the spine in better position. It will also prevent flexion or bending of the hip joints in the supine position. Patients often find bedboards uncomfortable for the first night or two but later discover that they are in less pain and feel more rested when using them.

Many patients will find it easier to get into and out of bed if the bed is raised 6 inches on blocks.

A patient with arthritis of the spine will do well to rest on his back with a small pillow or folded towel between his shoulder blades, but not under his head. Maintaining these optimum resting positions often becomes tiring after a while, and it is necessary to move to another position. It must be remembered, however, that the ideal resting position should be kept as long as possible.

Chair rest. When the patient is allowed up he should use a chair that is not too low. Most chairs should be raised 3 to 4 inches on blocks. With this added height the legs are not bent as much at the hips. The seat should be flat and the back high, broad, and uncurved. The height of the arms of a chair must be adjusted individually, depending upon the length of the patient's back and whether his arm and shoulders are affected.

Sitting in a chair for longer than an hour generally produces stiffness and fatigue. During the more acute stages of the disease, therefore, it is probably wiser to be up in a chair three to five times a day for shorter intervals than fewer times for longer periods. Whenever necessary, the patient should be assisted in getting out of a chair, so that he does not have to struggle to raise himself. Such activity puts undesirable strain on the legs and arms. An assistant will find it not too difficult to place his arms under the patient's arms and pull up and back, letting the patient's legs rather than his own back take the weight.

Avoidance of Pain

Pain will sap the patient's strength and energy. In arthritis, pain is largely a direct result of the disease, but some of it is the result of fatigue and poor posture. Much of such pain can be prevented. Almost any occupation performed for a long period will produce fatigue and pain.

The problem for most patients is that they do one thing too long. A change to something else will rest them. Automobile rides are often too long for arthritic patients. If they would stop once in a while to stretch and walk, they would be less tired at the end of the journey. A double-feature movie is too long for a patient to sit through because he is unable to change his position. Countless other examples could be mentioned.

The importance of maintaining good posture cannot be emphasized enough, and the patient should be impressed with the advantages of maintaining good posture. It is a personal daily responsibility that might be regarded as a nuisance and that many may neglect to carry out. Actually 20 to 30 minutes a day is time enough to carry out many of the fundamental postural exercises. If these are done day in and day out for months or years, a proper balance of muscle strength is built up which maintains a person in good posture without his even being aware of it. The patient must realize that he cannot expect results quickly: he may not see any improvement until six months have gone by. In one sense six months is a long time in a person's life. In another sense it is a very short time if, in that period, he learns to escape the pain and fatigue of poor posture.

Treatment of Traumatic Arthritis

Traumatic joint disease may result from severe blows or falls, or from trauma incident to poor posture, athletic activities, or various occupations. Traumatic arthritis is a frequent cause of prolonged disability following injury. The effect of trauma upon articular structures depends upon the type, severity, and duration of the injury as well as upon the reaction of the individual. The period between the injury and the production of traumatic arthritis may vary from days to several months. Pain and limitation of motion may persist for years following a single strain or contusion, even without obvious anatomic change.

According to one authority, preferred treatment regimens are composed of: rest and avoidance of any operative trauma; whichever method of heat gives relief of pain, or rotation of various types of heat; massage; exercise; correction of posture; use of properly fitted shoes and supports; exercises for the feet; weight reduction (if indicated); in some cases, the use of splints or roller bandages; and special corsets or braces.

If the affected joint is splinted, the splints should be used continuously during the acute phase of the disease, except for their removal once daily to permit several full painless motions of the joint to prevent the formation of dense adhesions.

BACK AILMENTS

Coccygodynia

Coccygodynia is a pathological condition that is usually caused by direct trauma to the coccyx, such as a fall or a kick that results in sprain of the sacrococcygeal ligaments. The pain is aggravated when the patient sits on a hard surface or rises from a sitting posture, and may be lessened by sitting on an air cushion or by contracting the gluteal muscles while sitting.

Treatment

If treated early, manipulation of the coccyx by inserting the index finger of one hand into the rectum and pressing against the back of the coccyx with the index finger of the other hand will sometimes give miraculous relief. Of course, this procedure should be carried out by a physician or surgeon. All patients with continued pain, especially on movement or after sitting for any length of time, should receive careful physical therapy before operative removal of the vertebrae is considered. Heat (diathermy is best for this condition), followed by massage, will usually relieve the pain temporarily. After a few treatments of this nature, manipulation of the coccyx by the physician may possibly permanently eliminate the painful condition.

If the coccyx has been fractured, diathermy should not be used for the relief of pain since it often aggravates the condition, even when the fracture has healed. In these cases it is better to employ moist packs or infrared therapy, followed by massage.

Low Back Pain

The general practitioner will have many occasions to treat pain in the lower back, a condition common to patients of all ages.

Differential Characteristics

1. Localized or generalized low back pain is the chief symptom of lumbosacral and sacroiliac strain.
2. Back pain on awakening in the morning but which rapidly improves after the patient becomes involved in the day's activities is characteristic of mild, chronic arthritis of the spine; it is due to the fact that the articulations become stiffened during rest but limber up as soon as one moves about.
3. A history of the patient's having been aware of something snapping or slipping in the back suggests a periosteal or ligamentous tear.
4. Recurring attacks of low lumbar backache with sciatica in the back of the leg are usually due to defective intervertebral disks; in most instances the pain is intensified by sneezing or coughing during periods of acute pain.
5. Spinal pain due to the presence of a neoplasm may be aggravated by immobilization. A metastatic malignancy may cause severe spinal pain that is not

Rest position. Breathe deeply, raising chest. Exhale by drawing upper abdomen in. Take next breath against uplifted chest. Repeat 10 times.

Tighten lower abdominal muscles. Relax. Repeat 10 times.

Flatten back against floor by tightening lower abdomen and buttocks at the same time. Relax. Repeat 10 times.

Hug both knees to chest. Repeat 10 times.

Hug one knee to chest. Raise other leg straight and lower slowly, keeping abdomen in. Repeat 5 times with each leg.

Pillow under abdomen, tighten buttocks. Relax. Repeat 10 times.

Figure 3. A set of useful exercises to relieve low back pain. (Adapted from a publication by Geigy Pharmaceuticals, in turn adapted from *Arthritis and Allied Conditions,* 8th ed., by Joseph L. Hollander and Daniel J. M Carty, Jr. [Lea and Febiger, 1972], and from *Home Care Programs Arthritis: A Manual for Patients* [Arthritis Foundation, 1969].)

relieved by rest on a rigid bed, or by braces, casts, or local heat, but only by opiates.

6. Pain that is definitely localized, but which does not radiate, may occur with fractures or abscesses of the vertebrae.

7. Pain that disappears during the night and increases during the following afternoon or evening as fatigue from daily activity sets in often occurs in patients with backaches that result from poor body posture.

Treatment

The patient with a back condition should rest lying in a supine position and sleep on a very firm mattress with a plywood board between the mattress and spring. Additional support to the lower back is often helpful; this may be in the form of taping, the use of a binder, or a pillow placed under the knees while flexing the hips.

Moist hot packs for 20 minutes, 3 to 4 times a day, as well as infrared heat therapy, may be used. Heat should not be applied continuously; neither should a heating pad be used all the time, or all night, since prolonged application of heat increases congestion, thereby defeating its purpose. Shortwave diathermy may be used. Some authorities advocate alternating the use of the various forms of heat therapy.

In acute cases massage should not be attempted, but later, as the acute stage subsides, very light massage which gradually becomes deeper may be indicated; the type used will depend on the degree of acuteness of the symptoms.

Corrective exercises for back pain are indicated only after the acute stage is over and the patient has become ambulatory, or after the symptoms have become milder. Since many different back exercises may be prescribed, it is often up to the therapist to instruct the patient in the type of exercises best suited to treating the particular condition. The following exercises are designed to strengthen the stomach muscles and stretch the contracted back muscles. The patient should begin by doing each exercise ten times twice a day and increase by one each day until he is doing each exercise 20 times twice a day.

Some pain during performance of the exercises is acceptable, but if the pain lasts for several days, the number of times the exercises are done should be reduced. The patient should be instructed to:

1. Lie on the back with a rolled blanket or a small pillow under the knees. With the hands up beside the head, tilt the pelvis to flatten the lower back on the table by pulling up and in with the lower abdominal muscles. Hold the back flat and breathe in and out easily, relaxing the upper abdominal muscles. (There should be good chest expansion during inspiration, but the back should not arch.)

2. Lie on the back. Bend the knees and place the feet flat on the table. With the hands up beside the head, tilt the pelvis to flatten the lower back on the table. Straighten the legs as much as possible with the back held flat. Keep the back flat and return the knees to bent position, sliding one leg back at a time.

3. Sit with legs extended forward. Place a rolled blanket under the knees to allow slight knee bend. Pull in with the abdominal muscles, keep the pelvis tilted back, and reach forward toward the toes, bending the lower back. The stretch should be felt in the lower back, not under the knees or in the upper back or neck.

4. Sit with knees straight. Reach forward toward the toes. Try to bend at the hip joints by tilting the pelvis forward. A stretch should be felt under the knees and along the hamstring muscles.

5. Lie on the abdomen and contract the glutei.

6. Lie on the abdomen and grasp the top of the bed with the hands. Raise one thigh. Raise both thighs at the same time.

7. Lie on the abdomen. Grasp the side of the bed with the hands. Raise one knee and cross it over the opposite one by rotating the lower part of the back. Keep the chest and shoulders flat. Move the other knee in the same manner.

8. Lie on the back and draw one knee up to the chest, bring it up tight with the hands, then return it slowly to the original position. Do not allow the knee to straighten out. Repeat with the other knee.

9. Lie on the back and draw one knee to the chest, then straighten that knee, pointing the leg upward as far as possible, flex the knee and return to original position. Alternate with the opposite leg, repeating this cycle 8 to 10 times.

When back pain is due to trauma, infection, or arthritis, an individualized program of rest, heat, massage, and exercise, as described above, can be helpful in relieving symptoms and correcting their cause. Pain that is due to protrusion of an intervertebral disk may be somewhat relieved by infrared heat or hot moist packs but these modalities will not remedy the cause, and diathermy may even aggravate the condition. Any form of treatment that increases pain should not be used.

An attempt should be made to restore the strength of the supporting muscles of the lower back, that is, the abdominal and gluteal muscles. A prosthetic back support may be indicated after the patient becomes ambulatory. If the symptoms are attributable to sacroiliac strain, the pelvis must be supported. The patient may also need to be taught exercises to correct some mechanical abnormality of the feet.

Lumbago

The term lumbago denotes an acutely painful back. Attacks usually come on suddenly, sometimes after some minor injury or, more often, after some unusual strain, perhaps from lifting, or after a change from a rather sedentary occupation to very active or heavy work. Lumbago may develop when a person cools off rapidly after being very warm or overheated.

When lumbago persists, treatment consists of rest, heat, and massage; often it yields best to infrared radiation. Diathermy is not recommended until after infrared therapy or hot packs have been tried.

The bed should be hard in order to avoid sagging of the buttocks.

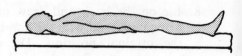

A hard, straight-back chair is desirable.

Lifting should be avoided. When unavoidable, the legs should do most of the work. The elbows can be supported by the thighs.

Figure 4. Hints for avoiding back strain. (Adapted from a publication by Geigy Pharmaceuticals, in turn adapted from *Arthritis and Allied Conditions,* 8th ed., by Joseph L. Hollander and Daniel J. McCarty, Jr. [Lea and Febiger, 1972], and from *Home Care Programs in Arthritis: A Manual for Patients* [Arthritis Foundation, 1969].)

Lumbosacral Strain

Strains on the back are usually caused by less severe injuries than those which result in sprains. Therefore, the signs and symptoms are less pronounced. However, failure on the part of the physician or patient to recognize a strain and to treat it as a potential troublemaker often results in prolonged disability. In most cases, the patient can remain ambulatory.

A firm binder should be applied and the patient should receive heat, massage, and graduated active exercise daily. Between treatments the patient should have a hot bath daily, followed by rest of at least 30 minutes before going out-of-doors. Should the symptoms grow worse, or if they are prolonged for more than a week, the patient should have a few days' rest and receive the treatment prescribed for sprains of the back (which see).

Sprains

Many accidents that are serious enough to cause a fracture are followed by sprain, although x-ray evidence will eliminate fracture as a cause. A sudden twist or fall when one is in a strained position often results in back sprain; for example, slipping while straining to lift a heavy object, or having a sudden weight thrown upon the straining body. A sprain will cause some tearing of ligaments and muscle attachments about the back, ecchymoses, minute hemorrhages, exudation, and swelling.

Pain is usually felt immediately, causing the person to cease his activity; however, after a few hours the pain may subside and he will return to work. Continued use of the back aggravates the condition and the next morning, or a day or two later, the pain becomes so severe that the patient cannot get out of bed or stand erect.

Treatment

It is extremely important for sprains to be diagnosed early and for the patient to be placed on bed rest. Most often these sprains are in the lower back — usually in the lumbosacral or sacroiliac area. They may not appear sufficiently serious to cause much concern, but allowing the patient to be up and around or to assume faulty posture in order to relieve his discomfort will only prolong the condition. On the other hand, allowing the patient to remain in bed for three or four weeks without massage or exercise will foster the formation of adhesions, painful joints, and other sequelae that are difficult to relieve.

Rest, heat, and massage for the first week, followed by graduated exercise to help restore function, will give relief to the majority of patients within three to four weeks. Strapping may be applied for two days to a week after the patient has become ambulatory, but, if possible, strapping should be avoided because it makes proper massage impossible. Sometimes a sacroiliac belt is indicated, but having the patient wear it indefinitely without removing it daily for massage only tends to doom him to invalidism; four to six weeks should be the limit for wearing such a belt.

In some cases, there has been good response to iontophoresis with procaine and with histamine.

Patients who do not respond to the treatments described above should be seen by an orthopedist. However, lack of response does not mean that physical therapy is contraindicated for sprains of the back.

BURSITIS

The first attack of bursitis can usually be relieved by physical therapy. The affected part should be placed at rest. An ice bag to the affected area will give more relief than heat, although infrared heat from a luminous source may be given for 30 minutes twice daily.

As the pain diminishes, careful massage and relaxed motion should be employed; later, active exercise is started. Acute subacromial, radiohumeral, olecranon, and prepatellar bursitis are treated in this manner.

Acute Subdeltoid Bursitis (Painful Shoulder Syndrome)

The subdeltoid bursa is the most frequent site of primary bursitis. Generally, it is the result of repeated mild trauma with the arm in an abducted position or a single injury in which the tendons attached to the greater tuberosity of the humerus are damaged, particularly when the fibers of the supraspinatus are injured.

The usual symptoms of acute subdeltoid bursitis are:

Agonizing pain in the region of the shoulder joint, aggravated by motion and becoming worse at night

At times, radiation of pain to the neck, arm, forearm, and insertion of the deltoid muscle

Limitation of motion and, in acute cases, extreme pain on even the slightest abduction or rotation

Tenderness around the greater tuberosity of the humerus just below the acromion process and, at times, over the entire shoulder

Sensitivity to pressure at the carotid process of the scapula and the bicipital groove of the humerus

Treatment

Any of the many available modalities may be utilized in treating the painful shoulder syndrome; if a certain one does not give relief, that does not necessarily mean that physical therapy is contraindicated.

In the very acute stage, ice packs or cold compresses and immobilization may be helpful. Diathermy or deep heat is not usually advisable during the early stages, since it may aggravate the condition. If ultrasonic therapy is used, the prescription should call for low intensity of 6 minutes duration for at least six to eight treatments. Iontophoresis with Novocain or potassium iodide has also been used for relief of pain.

After the very acute stage is over, diathermy or infrared heat may be used, followed by massage, and exercises should be started. Whether or not x-ray therapy or hydrocortisone is used, physical therapy modalities are helpful in the relief of pain and reestablishment of joint function.

Pendulum swinging

Bringing arm behind back

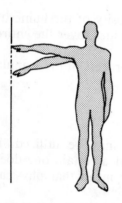

Climbing wall with fingers

Bringing arm overhead

Figure 5. Shoulder exercises for subdeltoid bursitis. (Adapted from a publication by Geigy Pharmaceuticals, in turn adapted from *Arthritis and Allied Conditions,* 8th ed., by Joseph L. Hollander and Daniel J. McCarty, Jr. [Lea and Febiger, 1972], and from *Home Care Programs in Arthritis: A Manual for Patients* [Arthritis Foundation, 1969].)

116

CERVICAL DISORDERS

Many pathological conditions that arise in the cervical region can be greatly helped by selected physical therapy modalities.

Whiplash injuries to the cervical spine are usually sustained by drivers or passengers in automobiles that are struck from the rear, the impact of which forcibly flexes and extends the neck. The injury may be mild to severe, appear immediately or within several weeks after the accident, and cause referred pain to various other parts of the body, such as the head, shoulders, and arms.

Arthritic changes in the cervical region are usually of osteoarthritic, rheumatic, or traumatic origin.

Muscular and ligamentous strain may be caused by poor posture or certain occupational factors.

Cervical disk injury is caused by the compression or irritation of one or more cervical nerves at the site of a protruding disk. The pain may radiate and be referred to the shoulder, arm, hand, or any part of the area supplied by the brachial plexus.

Treatment

Heat in the form of hot packs is a useful measure before applying traction. Massage is beneficial in relieving muscle spasm. The physician may inject a local anesthetic or prescribe certain drugs for the relief of pain. Correction of poor posture, immobilization, and the use of a cervical contour pillow are all helpful measures. Headache, including migraine, can be greatly helped by certain physical therapy modalities.

The patient with an acute cervical condition may be hospitalized, put into traction, and given such treatments as the physician prescribes. Traction has been used in the treatment of neck injuries for many decades. It may be applied continuously or intermittently. When correctly applied, continuous traction assures a certain amount of immobilization of the cervical spine, straightens it, and enlarges the intervertebral foramina to relieve compressive or irritative forces upon the nerve roots, and thus relieves muscle spasm. However, the conventional method of application by use of a head halter is not well tolerated because it causes discomfort in the chin and lower jaw. Also, the conventional weight of 5 to 10 pounds does nothing more than lift the weight of the head from the neck and keep the patient still to some extent.

The patient with a less acute cervical disorder is usually treated as an outpatient; physical therapy is especially beneficial in such cases.

CONTRACTURES

Contractures may result from atrophic changes in muscles and tendons. When any joint is maintained for an unduly long time in any one position, the muscles which ordinarily play a role in assuming that position shorten and limit motion in the opposite direction. This results in deformities.

Muscle shortening and consequent limitation of motion may also be caused by muscle imbalance due to spasticity and weakness.

Prevention

Proper positioning and regular periods of passive joint manipulation are of greatest value in preventing contractures. Cock-up splints for the hand, splints to counteract development of footdrop, encouraging motion in chronically ill persons who tend to assume positions leading to flexion contractures, and early use of therapy are all important in cases of fracture. When contractures are due to spasticity or muscle weakness, the use of splints, braces, and other devices to maintain deranged joints in more normal positions is helpful in preventing contractures.

Treatment

The chief treatment for contractures consists of stretching the involved muscles; for this treatment the patient must be completely relaxed in order to diminish interference by spasticity of the muscles involved. Other measures consist of heat, massage (active and passive), assistive exercises, whirlpool baths, continuous traction, and electric current that causes vigorous muscular contractions.

CONTUSIONS

Early treatment of bruised muscles and joints consists of the application of ice or cold compresses before the swelling starts and for as long as there is still danger of hemorrhage into the tissues. This will constrict the blood vessels and, together with the application of a well-padded compression bandage, will lessen ecchymosis, swelling, pain, tenderness, and limitation of motion. The injured part should be put at rest for 24 to 48 hours.

After the danger of hemorrhage is past, treatment consists of the daily application of infrared heat or diathermy, massage, and perhaps ultrasonics until the muscle or joint function returns to normal. The injured part should be protected by padding or strapping when the patient returns to work.

EPICONDYLITIS

Some authorities believe that epicondylitis, often referred to as tennis elbow, involves a true radiohumeral bursa, located between the common extensor muscle of the wrist and the radiohumeral joint of the elbow. This condition may follow effort requiring supination of the wrist against resistance (as in screw driving) or violent extension of the wrist with the hand pronated (as in playing tennis).

Pain over the lateral epicondyle of the humerus may be severe and may radiate to the outer side of the arm and forearm. Joint tenderness is present just distal to the lateral epicondyle. Pain is aggravated by dorsiflexion and supination of the wrist against resistance. Weakness of the wrist in dorsiflexion is pronounced. In obscure cases the diagnosis may be established by infiltration of the area about the lateral epicondyle with 1% procaine, which completely relieves all symptoms and signs. (This procedure is carried out by the physician.)

Treatment

Immobilization in a splint or by adhesive strapping with the wrist dorsiflexed and supinated, plus daily diathermy, is often successful. Recently, excellent results have been obtained with the use of ultrasonic therapy. Therapy may be required from four to six weeks.

FIBROMYOSITIS

Fibromyositis is a term applied to a group of nonspecific illnesses characterized by pain, tenderness, and stiffness of the joints, muscles, or adjacent structures. It may be acute or chronic and usually is secondary to trauma, infection, strain, poisons, or exposure to damp or cold.

Sudden onset of pain, which is aggravated by motion, is usual. Tenderness may be present and even localized to small "trigger" nodules. Local muscle spasm is noted in some cases. Other signs and symptoms will depend on the area involved. The condition tends to disappear completely in a few days but may occasionally become chronic or recur at frequent intervals. Before arriving at a diagnosis of chronic fibromyositis, all specific causes must be excluded, such as arthritis, bursitis, rheumatic fever, scleroderma, lupus erythematosus disseminatus, trichiniasis, and myositis ossificans. It may be necessary to observe a patient for several months before a diagnosis can be made.

Treatment

Relief may be obtained by such measures as rest, heat, massage, the administration of salicylates or muscle relaxant drugs (must be ordered by the physician), and the external use of various liniments. The injection (by the physician) of a 1% solution of procaine hydrochloride into the "trigger" nodules may be beneficial. The use of splints or a bedboard may sometimes be necessary.

FIBROSITIS

Fibrositis is a condition characterized by pain, stiffness, aching, and soreness in areas of the body containing fibrous tissue. Although a distinct entity, it ordinarily occurs in combination with either myalgia, in which there is simple muscular pain, or myositis, which is a nonsuppurative inflammation of muscle tissue. In fibrositis the inflammation is similar to that in myositis, but it is the connective tissue components of the muscles and joints that are involved. Any of the fibromuscular tissues in the body may be involved, but those of the back (lumbago), neck (torticollis), shoulders and thorax (pleurodynia), and thighs (charleyhorse) are especially affected. There are practically no physical findings except occasional fibrous nodules of varying size in the affected region.

Treatment

In the acute stage, when there is severe pain, the usual treatment for myositis consists of infrared radiation or hot packs for 20 minutes, twice daily. After the acute stage has subsided, diathermy may be given cautiously, accompanied by massage. The most important treatment after the acute stage is heavy local massage, which actually breaks up and disperses the fibrotic nodules.

Since the body parts are still tender at this stage of fibrositis, the massage must be applied gently at first to get rid of the exudation and relieve tension. Gradually much firmer pressure should be used and, as a rule, the pain will be relieved in a few days. The patient should be told beforehand that the massage will be painful and that pain will remain for a few hours after the treatment. General massage is of no value and mere rubbing of the skin is of no use whatsoever. The massage must be specifically directed to any palpable thickenings and to painful regions, great care being taken not to use too much pressure at first. After a few days, the congestion and exudation are eliminated and the fibrous thickenings become defined; many of them are detected only then. Massage should be applied every other day, or three times weekly for about 15 minutes. Length of treatment varies from one or two weeks to six or seven weeks, rarely longer, before complete relief is obtained. When an induration can be compressed against a bony part, more effective pressure can be exerted and the nodule is more rapidly broken down than it is when deeply buried among fleshy muscles. Exercise should be of the kind that stretches the muscles and other structures involved.

FRACTURES

No physician who treats fractures can truthfully say that he does not employ physical therapy. The prescription of heat at one time or another, in one form or another, is practically universal; so is home massage and exercise. The purpose of this discussion is to describe the action and effect of various physical therapy modalities on the pathologic and reparative changes that occur in fractures.

Injury to the Soft Tissues in Fractures

A common mistake in treating fractures is to concentrate only on the injury to the bone and to overlook the accompanying injury to the adjacent soft parts or tissues. To fracture a bone requires a considerable amount of force. The violence may occur directly in the form of a blow or crush, in which case the first effect of the force is expended upon the soft structures before reaching the bones, or indirectly, as by bending or twisting a part beyond its normal limits of elasticity, in which instance the giving way of the bone is accompanied by laceration of the overlaying soft parts. Severe strain is often imparted to the ligaments as well, sometimes at a point rather remote from the fracture.

Treatment

Between the time when — in a recently reduced fracture — the first cautious attempts at movement are begun and the later period when the bones have healed and vigorous exercises can be prescribed, lies an interval, often of many weeks, during which every detail of treatment must be managed with skill. This is when competent physical therapy pays off. The goal of all fracture treatment is complete restoration of function in the injured part in the shortest possible time. When the injury is of such a nature as to cause irreparable damage, the aim must be to minimize loss of function, particularly to try to avoid disabilities that would prevent the patient's return to his previous major activity. A perfect result implies that the involved part functions as well after injury as it did before.

The first step in treating a fracture is the reduction of it; after that, treatment consists of measures to achieve healing of the fracture and restoration of function of the part involved. Of all of the measures employed in treating fractures, by far the most important are two that are mutually antagonistic — rest and movement. Rest or immobilization is necessary to maintain reduction of the fracture and to allow healing of the bones; equally necessary from the standpoint of muscles, joints, blood vessels, and nerves is movement or mobilization to maintain and restore function.

Mobilization

Mobilization, or movement, stimulates the circulation, aids in the absorption of edema and other products of inflammation, restores the flexibility of the joints, frees the muscles from adhesions, overcomes atrophy, and restores strength.

Passive movement is motion that is performed without either active help or resistance from the patient's muscles. To secure complete muscular relaxation, however, the patient's metal cooperation is required. Obtaining this from a patient with a fractured extremity is an art that demands the maximum of patience and gentleness from the physical therapist. Gentle stroking massage has an important role in preparing the way and obtaining relaxation. The slightest jar or sudden movement will cause the patient's muscles to tighten and harmful resistive motion will be substituted for beneficial passive movement.

Active (free) movement is performed entirely by the patient's own muscles without assistance or resistance in either flexion or extension. The influence of gravity upon the movement is eliminated as completely as possible by supporting the part on a smooth hard surface in such a position that both flexion and extension are performed in a horizontal plane. Active movement is chiefly indicated as a transition from passive to resisted movements, at the time when healing has progressed to the point of consolidation but when the callus is still soft and requires protection; such exercise provides support for both segments of the limb, protects the fracture, reduces the amount of work to be done by the muscles, and, at the same time, permits free voluntary movement.

Resistive exercises are intended to build up strength in weak muscles by increasing the amount of work to be done. They may be performed either by requiring the patient to make a movement which is resisted manually by the physical therapist or by having the physical therapist move the joint while the patient resists. Resistive exercises may also be given with the aid of mechanical apparatus, the purpose being to increase the amount of work done by certain muscles.

Assistive movement is performed by active contraction of the patient's own muscles but with outside assistance of one kind or another. The assistance given may vary from gentle support of the weight of the limb by the physical therapist (producing an effect similar to that of free motion) to a considerable force exerted by the therapist which supplements the patient's muscles in overcoming a contracture or stretching fibrous adhesions. Instead of the manual aid, apparatus such as a weight and pulley or dumbbells may be employed. Gentle assistive motion is given in the early stage of fracture treatment, strong assistive motion in the later stages.

Massage

Only three types of massage are of value in the treatment of fractures: superficial stroking, effleurage, and kneading. Pain is always to be regarded as a warning signal; massage that is painful is also harmful.

Massage of recent fractures: Superficial stroking is the only type of massage employed for the treatment of fresh fractures to relieve pain, secure muscular relaxation, overcome swelling, and benefit the circulation. Massage is necessarily limited by the type and location of the fracture. To derive the most benefit from massage, the entire surface of the limb should be exposed to treatment. Limbs with loose, displaced fractures cannot be handled without jeopardizing the reduced position of the fragment. Whether massage should be given or not in a recent fracture is the decision of the physician or surgeon. The treatment must be given by an experienced physiotherapist. Superficial stroking can be perfected only by practice. The movement must be slow, gentle, and rhythmical, and made with the flat of the fingers, the hand being relaxed so as to adapt and mold itself to the part.

Massage in later treatment: When union is solid enough to permit the temporary or complete removal of the splint, deeper pressure may be permitted. Deep stroking massage (effleurage), supplemented occasionally by kneading, may then be employed to aid in restoring vasomotor tone and to help drain the clogged lymphatic system and empty surplus fluid from the tissue spaces. Since the action of effleurage is mechanical rather than reflex, it should be administered only in the centripetal direction, beginning with the tissues of the proximal portion of the extremity and emptying these, then proceeding a little distally and working back again over the proximal region, and repeating this maneuver as many times as necessary until the entire extremity has been treated.

While effleurage is classed as deep stroking massage and requires deep pressure, this does not mean hard or forcible pressure. The main requirement for proper administration of effleurage is muscular relaxation. As long as the muscles are hard and contracted, even the most vigorous pressure would scarcely be able to produce any deep effect. On the other hand, when the muscles are relaxed, the tissues transmit gentle, even pressure to the depths as though they were a fluid medium. Light, superficial stroking should always be employed to relax the muscles before proceeding with deep stroking; even after this has been begun, when certain regions are found to be hard instead of soft, one should return to the superficial stroking until these muscles have relaxed.

Heat

Heat is very useful in the treatment of fractures. Its physiological effects are the temporary production of vascular dilatation in the part and more rapid and abundant circulation of the blood. Heat has soothing and relaxing effects and should, therefore, be used before massage and mobilization.

The most convenient and generally used means of applying heat is the electric baker. The radiant heat lamp may also be used, as may the infrared lamp.

The whirlpool bath is one of the best physical therapy modalities to use in fracture cases because it combines the effects of heat and gentle massage. For fractures that involve the distal parts of the extremities, active exercises during the whirlpool bath will help in overcoming stiffness and in restoring function. Contrast baths, that is, alternate soaking in hot and cold water, are also helpful.

Diathermy and short-wave diathermy are not usually used as a source of heat in treating fractures. If diathermy is used, it should be at a very low current and a short duration. It should not be used at all in fractures that have been set by open reduction or those in which any metal pins or plates were used.

Treatment of Colles' Fracture

Colles' fracture of the wrist is a common injury that often occurs when one tries to catch himself when falling. The fracture is evaluated by determining the range of motion possible and testing for muscle strength.

During the fixation period, treatment involves exercises to all free joints including:

Shoulder movements, particularly rotation

Elbow movements — flexion and extension: pronation and supination may or may not be ordered

Finger and thumb movements should be conscientiously practiced by the patient and include such exercises as sq ieezing a small rubber ball or crumpling pieces of paper

Treatment following removal of the plaster cast includes:

Whirlpool bath, with wrist exercises being performed while the arm is in the water

Massage

Active assistive progressing to active resistive exercises of the hand and wrist; for example, turning a doorknob, wringing a cloth, and making a fist

HAND INJURIES

The treatment of injuries of the hand is a common and challenging problem in the general practice of medicine. Since any injury interferes with the functioning of the hand, serious and immediate treatment of injuries is imperative. Physical therapy has an integral and important part in whatever remedial program is undertaken. The guiding principles are similar in all types of injury — fracture, burn, laceration, or infection.

Treatment

Following a hand injury, physical therapy may be used during both the acute stage of treatment, in which the disturbance to the vascular system (as evidenced by edema) should be controlled, and during the recovery period, during which prevention of deformity and restoration of lost function are the main concerns of the therapist.

Movement should be started at the earliest possible moment, except when it might interfere with the healing of a fracture or soft tissue laceration, or when the resolution of an inflammatory process might be delayed. In some hand injuries early movement is impossible because of edema, pain, or splintage.

As the hand improves, the patient should be taught how to produce static contractions which will develop into active movements. Reeducation in the use of fine coordinating movements necessary for proper use of the hand requires much time and perseverence. These movements should be explained to the patient so he can understand the aims of the treatment.

Rehabilitative Therapy

After the acute effects of the trauma have subsided, the disability of the hand is thoroughly checked and methods of treatment are worked out to suit the individual case. It is important to secure the full cooperation of the patient because certain phases of the rehabilitation procedures are painful.

Active movement is most important in the restoration of lost hand movements. Passive stretching and manipulation of the small joints of the hand have absolutely no place in the treatment program; in most cases further loss of function will result from these procedures since any force applied will tear the tissues, which will heal by forming more scar tissue, itself a barrier to movement. Active movement may consist of either exercises or occupational therapy designed to restore the lost function of the hand.

Radiant heat or an infrared lamp may be used to relax the muscles before starting active movements. Paraffin baths are also an excellent modality to use in preparing the hand for treatment. When edema develops following a severe injury such as a burn, the positive pole of the direct galvanic current may be used to control swelling in addition to other methods of treatment ordered by the physician. Massage may be given if there is no infection or dermatologic disorder.

Exercises are frequently prescribed. The importance of relaxation should be explained to the patient before exercises are begun. He should make every effort to relax all muscle groups and fatigue must be avoided. Tired muscles go into spasm which is undesirable at all stages of the treatment.

Passive exercises consist of bending and straightening the patient's fingers. This is done by the therapist while the patient allows his fingers to be relaxed. These movements should never be forced.

Active exercises are performed by the patient and are done according to the following instructions:

1. Palm flat on the table, raise and lower fingers one by one.
2. Make an "O" by touching thumb to finger tips one at a time.
3. Crumple a sheet of newspaper into a small ball with one hand.
4. Squeeze a small rubber ball or sponge.
5. Pick up coins or buttons of assorted sizes.
6. Keep time to music with finger (drum with extended finger).
7. Rest hand on table; spread fingers wide and then bring them together.
8. Flip balls of paper with fingers, or flip a lightweight book or folded newspaper off extended fingers.
9. Place hands with palms together in front of chest; push against fingers of affected hand with fingers of the uninjured hand.

MYOSITIS

Myositis, or inflammation of the muscles, is characterized by aching pain in affected muscles, which are tender to pressure and held rigid in order to prevent movement. Myositis has certain sites of predilection, such as the shoulder muscles, muscles of the lumbar region (lumbago), intercostal muscles (pleurodynia), and the posterior muscles of the neck (torticollis).

Treatment

Treatment in acute cases consists of physiological rest and the local application of heat followed by gentle massage.

In chronic cases, treatment is directed to the removal of

the products of inflammation through increasing the circulation by the application of infrared heat or diathermy, together with massage. When painful nodules are located, they should be manipulated or stretched; the patient should be told that this may involve considerable pain and discomfort. In stubborn cases of myositis large doses of negative galvanic current have proved beneficial.

OSTEOARTHRITIS (DEGENERATIVE JOINT DISEASE)

Treatment

Rest

Rest is an important part of the therapy program for osteoarthritis. Rest may be local or general, depending upon the parts involved. Since overuse of affected joints is thought to bring about the symptoms and may be a factor in producing further damage, complete rest may appear more rational; this is not practical for most patients, however, and it is probably not necessary. When an acute, severe exacerbation of the symptoms occurs, particularly in the knees, hips, or spine, absolute bed rest for a few days may be the most rapid means of relieving the pain. Unfortunately, many patients are obsessed with the thought that they must exercise the affected parts continuously to prevent stiffness. Nothing could be farther from the truth; excessive exercise results in additional trauma and damage to the involved parts. Any movement that tends to throw strain upon the affected joints should be eliminated insofar as possible. The joints should, however, be moved through a full range of motion several times a day.

Heat

Most patients with degenerative joint disease benefit symptomatically if heat, massage, and exercise are used. One form of heat may be as effective as another. The doctor's choice of infrared, baker, diathermy, paraffin bath, hot fomentations, or any other form of heat may depend on the patient's response to one or another type. The effect of any of these modalities is to produce an increased blood supply in the area treated.

Heat may be applied daily or several times a day if the symptoms are marked. Painful Heberden's nodes (small nodes that form at the distal interphalangeal articulations) may be relieved by bathing the hands in hot Epsom salt solution. Paraffin baths are also used very successfully for hands. The length of any of the heat treatments will vary from 20 to 30 minutes.

Massage

Massage of the entire limb and involved joint is usually recommended. Massage of the intervening muscles may be rather vigorous so that muscular atrophy does not occur; massage of the joint itself should consist of light stroking movements for the first several days. More pressure may be exerted later if pain and swelling of the joint are not aggravated. Care must be taken to avoid massage of the tender bony tissue coverings, since such irritation may cause swelling and sensitiveness.

Exercise

Exercise of the involved joint is important to prevent the formation of fibrous adhesions in the neighborhood of the joint and to decrease the tendency to atrophy in the surrounding muscles. These exercises must be performed in moderation and should not be so severe as to cause further injury to the joint. Patients should not constantly keep their joints on the move. Too much or too vigorous exercise may increase joint stiffness. Any pain or discomfort that remains for more than one to two hours following exercise indicates that the exercise was too severe. Active exercise is preferred to passive exercise.

Treatment of Degenerative Cervical Joint Disease

For osteoarthritis of the cervical spine, diathermy, massage, and graded exercises may be used, accompanied by manual traction or suspension with gentle rotation to overcome the crowding of structures in the neck that causes pain from bony hypertrophy, muscular spasm, and thinning of the intervertebral disks.

Cervical traction, using Sayre apparatus or its various modifications, is a valuable procedure in the treatment of cervical osteoarthritis. In addition, it may sometimes have diagnostic value in clarifying the nature of indefinite symptoms referable to the neck, shoulder, and arm. After the patient has had several treatments and instruction in the use of cervical traction, it usually can be carried out satisfactorily at home. A felt head sling that conforms to the patient's measurements is used. The patient produces the desired degree of traction by flexing his knees. (See pages 64–65 for instructions for applying cervical traction.)

OSTEOMYELITIS, CHRONIC

Many physical therapy modalities are available to the physician for treating the patient with chronic osteomyelitis.

Heat will improve the blood and lymph supply and will also relieve pain. Diathermy may be used but it must be a mild application; an exposure of 15 to 20 minutes is sufficient. Infrared and luminous radiation may be used over open lesions. Ultraviolet radiation of the sinuses leading to the bone also stimulates the growth of granulation tissue.

PAINFUL FEET

Several common physical therapy modalities may be tried before the patient with painful feet is referred to an orthopedist.

In some acute cases, rest for a few days, felt pads, adhesive strapping, simple foot exercises, attention to proper posture and gait, correctly fitted shoes, and hot and cold contrast baths will help greatly. Special exercises for the feet, which can be given by any therapist, will be found on pages 71–72 and 76–77 and the contrast bath technique is described on pages 51–52.

ROTATOR CUFF SYNDROME

The rotator (musculotendinous) cuff is made up of fibers of the supraspinatus, infraspinatus, teres minor, and suprascapularis muscles, which blend with and reinforce the capsule of the shoulder joint. The rotator cuff syndrome is caused by damage to these fibers and is characterized by pain and interference with normal shoulder movement.

Treatment

Treatment for the rotator cuff syndrome is based on an evaluation of the degree of interference with range of motion of the shoulder joint and the results of muscle tests.

The objectives of physical therapy in this condition are to relieve pain, augment the healing process, and protect the cuff from further damage. Modalities used to achieve these objectives are heat, ultrasound, and exercise. The application of heat helps to relieve the pain that occurs in the acute stage of the disorder and stimulates healing. Ultrasound is also used for this purpose. When the pain has subsided, the patient should practice the shoulder exercises described on page 98. As an alternative to the treatment outlined above, cold may be used instead of heat for the relief of pain.

SOFT TISSUE INJURIES

Traumatic injuries to muscle and fibrous tissue are treated according to the degree and extent of the injury. In extensive and severe injury, the initial treatment should consist of rest and cold applications, followed by some form of heat — hot compresses, hot baths, alternating applications of heat and cold, whirlpool baths, radiant heat, or diathermy. These measures promote absorption of effusions and relieve pain, and thus help to prevent atrophy resulting from disuse. The absorption of extravasated lymph or blood may be further accelerated by massage.

In the early stages it might be necessary to limit the range of motion of the injured part. Later, assistive and voluntary exercise will facilitate restoration of normal function of the injured part. Muscle contraction, stimulated first by galvanic and later by interrupted current, helps promote healing. To secure prompt relief of pain and spasm following injuries, procaine iontophoresis may be used. Ethyl chloride spray by a special technique may also be used in conjunction with movements of the affected part. (For injuries to soft tissues in cases of fracture, see page 122.)

SPRAINS

Straining or tearing of the ligaments around a joint occurs in varying degrees, and treatment varies according to the damage done to the surrounding soft tissues. For example, immediate walking may be advised in the case of a slight sprain of the ankle, while bed rest may be advised in cases of severe sprain.

When ligaments are torn and muscles, blood vessels, nerves, tendons, and the synovial membranes of the joint are injured, there will be hemorrhage from the torn vessels and muscle spasm. Immediate treatment therefore consists of the local application of cold for one or two hours, rest, elevation of the part, and the use of a well-padded compression bandage. After the first 24 hours, treatment includes the daily application of external heat or diathermy followed by massage, the use of an elastic bandage, and ultrasonic therapy. When the ankle or wrist joint is involved, whirlpool baths are very helpful. Good results have been obtained from Novocain iontophoresis.

A mild sprain of the ankle can be treated satisfactorily by strapping that prevents lateral motion but permits plantar and dorsal flexion, which, it is thought, promotes the return of circulation to the part and prevents the formation of adhesions.

STIFF AND ANKYLOSED JOINTS

Stiff joints may benefit from the use of radiant heat or hot packs followed by massage, even when there is fairly severe ankylosis, if such applications are followed by stretching and exercise. In less severe cases, such therapy should lead to complete restoration of function. Treatments should be given daily for four to six weeks and the effects carefully checked before forced manipulation under anesthesia or a more radical surgical procedure is attempted. Diathermy is not recommended for stiff and ankylosed joints.

SYNOVITIS

Any trauma directed at a joint, such as a blow, wrench, twist, or any forced movement beyond the normal range of motion, or the overuse of an abnormal joint, may result in a synovitis if the trauma is severe enough to produce a disturbance in the synovial membrane. The characteristic signs are the presence of fluid in the joint, muscle spasm and pain, and limitation of motion. Usually there are also signs or symptoms of some extra-articular injury or injury of adjacent soft parts.

Treatment

The primary consideration in the treatment of acute synovitis is rest, with the affected part in the position allowing greatest relaxation of the adjacent muscles, thus preventing further muscle spasm and pain. Inasmuch as the trauma may often cause hemorrhagic synovitis, aspiration of the fluid by the physician, followed by an application of heat — either by hot packs, moist compresses, or infrared or radiant heat — will frequently be enough to reduce the pain and muscular spasm. Diathermy may be used later on; if it aggravates the condition it should be discontinued.

Galvanic and faradic stimulation of the affected muscles, if there is much loss of muscle tone or relaxation of ligaments, will help to restore the integrity of the joint, as will light massage.

Motion should be urged from the beginning, at first passive and very light, and later active and increasing in range.

For synovitis of the knee or ankle, treatment includes the application of faradic current, which hastens the absorption of the accumulated fluids as it passes through the joint and produces quick results both in the relief of pain and the reduction of edema.

Traumatic Synovitis of the Knee

Traumatic synovitis of the knee with effusion is seen frequently in modern physical therapy departments where industrial injuries are treated. Treatment for this condition consists of:

1. Application of cold compresses to the joint for 24 to 48 hours, if much effusion is present.
2. Heat to the upper portion of the thigh, mild and not too prolonged at first, followed on the second or third day by gentle massage of the upper third of the thigh.
3. Quadriceps-setting exercises to prevent atrophy of this muscle.
4. Application of some form of heat to the knee as the swelling subsides; heat must be mild and not too prolonged at first.
5. Assistive active motions (not causing pain); lateral and rotatory movements must be avoided. Between these treatments the knee is immobilized by an adhesive strapping with additional protection by felt pads placed laterally.
6. Early restoration of motion with the aid of strapping and crutches, to prevent atrophy of the thigh muscles.
7. Resistive exercises, after heavier massage has been used and pain is lessened. These exercises may be performed by the patient sitting on the edge of a table and resisting extension of the affected leg by crossing the other foot in front of it, or by using various weights to offer resistance to motion of the quadriceps.

TENOSYNOVITIS

Tenosynovitis is an inflammation of a tendon sheath; its presence is first recognized by the patient not so much on account of pain, which is usually slight, but because of a feeling of weakness when he attempts to bring the tendon into use. Palpable and audible creaking (crepitus) may be noted when the tendon is active. When effusion of any amount takes place, visible swelling occurs along the tendon and the crepitus ceases. In chronic cases, especially when infection has occurred, granulation tissue forms within the sheath, firm adhesions develop, and pain and interference with free action result. The tendons most commonly affected are those of the wrist, thumb, and ankle.

Treatment

Treatment of tenosynovitis includes:

Rest of the part involved (very important)

Avoidance of activities that cause pain

Application of infrared or luminous heat for 30 minutes twice a day. Application of light splints if the patient does not respond to the three measures listed above

Adhesive plaster strapping for fixation of the ankle, fingers, or wrist, made to be removable so that heat can be applied to the part

Later, local heating by whirlpool or paraffin baths followed by mild massage, which will tend to soften and break up the exudate resulting from inflammation if it is not too densely concentrated

Ultrasonic therapy, for which good results have been reported and which can be given in conjunction with any other physical therapy modality

Avoidance of massage

TORTICOLLIS

Torticollis, the syndrome of acute painful stiff neck, is characterized by severe pain and extreme rigidity of the neck muscles and is usually associated with some degree of tilting of the head. There is usually a very definite trigger point which, when palpated, sets off a painful reaction. The causes of this syndrome include sudden sprains, strains, twists, and other injuries. However, the most common cause is a draft of cold air on the unprotected neck during sleep or while in a prolonged, relatively immobile posture, such as driving a car with the side window open and cold air constantly blowing on the neck.

Treatment

Diathermy followed by massage, infrared therapy or hot packs, and, sometimes, ultrasonic therapy are very helpful in relieving the pain and spasm of torticollis. If massage with a counterirritant is used, better results are obtained. Ethyl chloride spray sometimes provides relief from pain and stiffness. An important aspect of the treatment includes protection of the neck muscles and nerves from further injury.

TOTAL KNEE REPLACEMENT

Physical therapy treatment following total knee replacement consists primarily of exercises and measures to restore joint function.

The patient is instructed to perform the following exercises while lying on his back in bed:

1. With the ankle resting on a towel roll, tighten the muscle that extends the knee (quadriceps); hold for 5 seconds; relax.
2. Raise the leg as high as possible, keeping the knee straight; then lower the leg slowly to the surface of the bed.
3. Slide the foot up toward the hip with the knee bent as much as possible; then slide the foot back down on the surface of the bed.
4. With the thigh resting on a towel roll placed close to the knee, lift the knee off the surface to straighten it; hold for 5 seconds; relax.
5. With the knee resting on a two-towel roll so that it is bent and the foot rests on the surface of the bed, place

sandbags or weight boot on foot; lift foot to straighten the knee; then lower foot and leg to surface of the bed.

The patient is also instructed to perform the following two exercises while sitting in a firm chair with a towel roll under his knee:

1. Raise foot to straighten knee; lower foot toward floor and move it back under the chair to flex the knee as much as possible (the hips must remain firmly on the chair, no leaning).
2. Prop foot on footstool so knee is slightly flexed (45°); place hand sandbags over ankle or place weight boot on foot and lift to straighten knee; then lower foot and weight to the stool; repeat five times, twice a day. Gradually increase the weight used, starting with 3 pounds and working up to a total of 30 pounds.

18
NEUROLOGIC DISORDERS

The neurologic conditions discussed here are those most commonly seen by the general practitioner. As the demands on the physician to restore patients to maximum economic and social effectiveness increase, he turns more and more to the physical therapist for help in carrying out rehabilitative procedures. Many of the recommended procedures can be carried out in the home as well as in a hospital setting.

BELL'S PALSY

Among the cervical nerve lesions that cause conditions requiring physical therapy, Bell's palsy (facial nerve paralysis) is the one most commonly seen by the general practitioner.

General Treatment

The facial muscle test and electrodiagnosis are both used in evaluating the condition and deciding on the treatment modalities to be used. The usual treatment program includes:

Massage
Electrical stimulation (most valuable during the first six weeks after onset of the paralysis)
Muscle reeducation
Application of a facial splint to help prevent stretching and contracture of muscles
Guarding against overstretching of the muscles on the paralyzed side of the face by instructing patient against excessive laughing and smiling

If the treatment outlined above does not result in

improvement within two weeks after the onset of the paralysis, further electrodiagnostic studies may provide information that will enable the physician to prognose the final outcome. Studies should include the test for reaction of degeneration (see p. 35) and the chronaxy test. In chronaxy testing, a current that has a known contractile effect upon an individual muscle or nerve is applied. Since the difference in time necessary to get a contraction is the only variable factor, this time can be accurately observed and recorded by a chronaxy meter.

At-Home Treatment

Infrared heat or warm moist Turkish towels should be applied to the affected area for 15 minutes, followed by gentle stroking massage for 10 minutes. Then the patient should try the following exercises in front of a mirror. In order not to exaggerate the exercises on the unparalyzed side of the face, the patient should limit the movement by placing his hand on that side of the face. The exercises should be done ten times twice a day.

1. Raise eyebrows and wrinkle forehead.
2. Frown, bringing eyebrows together and then down.
3. Close eyelids tightly.
4. Wrinkle nose as if expressing distaste.
5. Grimace, drawing corners of mouth down and to the sides.
6. Draw corners of mouth downward strongly.
7. Purse or pucker the lips.
8. Protrude upper lip.
9. Protrude lower lip.
10. Blow.
11. Smile.
12. Press lower jaw down against hand.
13. Close jaws tightly.
14. Move lower jaw forward and to the side, first right, then left.

Outpatient Treatment

In addition to continuing treatment at home, the patient should regularly visit the physician's office or the outpatient department of a hospital to receive electrical stimulation when excessive sagging of facial muscles is manifested. If the paralysis is mild, faradic or sinusoidal current may be used. Electrical stimulation should be given daily for one week, then three times weekly for a few months or until there is an indication that voluntary motion is returning. As soon as there is some sign of recovery, the electrical treatments should be discontinued.

BRACHIAL NEURITIS

The chief complaint of the patient with brachial neuritis is local or referred pain and limitation of arm movements. The pain is usually localized in the region of distribution of the fourth, fifth, and sixth cervical nerves, or it may be referred to the hand, especially to the fifth finger, or to the thumb and index finger.

Treatment

The patient should remain in bed in the recumbent position. Cervical traction should be applied using the bindings of a canvas or flannel head halter, a spreader, and a rope that goes over a pulley and from which a weight of 4 to 12 pounds is suspended. The head of the bed should be elevated about 8 inches to allow the patient's body to furnish countertraction to the weight.

Application of an ointment or lotion containing an anodyne, and hot packs or fomentations protected with a warm, dry, flannel covering have been found to be beneficial. The patient's neck and shoulders should be protected from dampness and drafts.

Daily treatments that utilize such modalities as mild infrared heat and very mild massage should be used.

At the end of a variable period, some orthopedists recommend that patients wear a neck brace. Physical therapy is continued, with the brace being removed during treatments.

CEREBRAL VASCULAR ACCIDENT

The patient who has had a cerebral vascular accident (CVA, stroke) resulting in hemiplegia is often treated with physical therapy to prevent or correct deformity, to improve his motor function, and to help him develop ability to carry out the activities of daily living to the extent that he can, at least partially, take care of his personal needs.

While the patient is still bedridden certain simple tests can be utilized to determine the degree to which his motor functions can be restored. If he can move his arm on the affected side, he will probably be able to learn to walk again, since the arm is almost always more severely affected than the leg. If he is able to raise the affected leg one inch off the bed while in the supine position, he probably has sufficient power remaining to permit walking.

Treatment

Treatment should be instituted as soon as possible. In most cases, it can be started within the first week after the stroke. Medical contraindications to the early use of physical therapy are few, and it is important that daily passive movements be given to the involved extremities very early in the course of treatment.

Numerous modalities and technics, which may be used singly or in combination, are available and helpful to the physician in his management of hemiplegic patients. The more commonly used modalities include heat of many types, sedative or stimulating massage, electric stimulation, movement reeducation, exercises, and training in the use of such apparatus as walkers, braces, crutches, canes, and splints.

Early Measures to Prevent Deformity

Four simple procedures that can be carried out during the acute stage of illness and while the patient is still bedridden will help to prevent some of the deformities commonly seen in hemiplegic patients:

1. A small pillow placed in the axilla on the affected side will help prevent adduction of that arm toward the shoulder.
2. A footboard or posterior leg splint applied to the affected leg will prevent toe drop and shortening of the tendon of Achilles.
3. Sandbags placed along the lateral surface of the affected leg will help prevent outward rotation of the leg.
4. Practicing quadriceps setting early will maintain and improve muscle strength needed for ambulation later.

Heat Therapy

Indications for the use of external heat are pain, spasticity, and edema. Many patients obtain relief from moist hot packs. The application of heat should be followed by massage whenever edema is present.

Electrical Stimulation

When flaccidity persists, electrical stimulation will sometimes help to maintain muscle tone and prevent atrophy. Spastic muscles should never be stimulated.

Exercise

Exercise is a very important part of the treatment in hemiplegia. The type of exercise used will, of course, depend on the condition of the patient's affected extremities. Various types of movement can be used — active, passive, assistive, and resistive — as well as muscle education and reeducation.

The physical therapist and the patient should both be before a mirror when the therapist demonstrates an exercise, and it will be helpful for the patient to always perform his exercises before a mirror. The physical therapist must watch the exercising patient closely and not allow him to continue until he becomes fatigued, breathless, or dizzy.

The patient should be allowed to use the unaffected limb to assist the affected one only when motion is impossible without assistance.

Slow passive movements of the affected extremities and encouragement of active movement of all extremities should be started as soon as possible after the most acute stage of illness is over. Special attention should be given to the upper extremities.

The following suggestions for active exercise will help to prevent the development of contractures and deformities.

1. Flex the fingers; try to touch the thumb with each finger; extend and spread the fingers; make a fist.
2. Flex and extend the wrist; flex the elbow and try to touch the shoulder; extend the arm and bring it to the side.
3. Use the unaffected hand to lift the affected one to the head, to the opposite side, and back.
4. Flex, extend, and spread the toes; dorsiflex the feet; flex and extend the knees. This strengthens weak muscles and stretches spastic ones.
5. Grasp and hold objects of various sizes; lift objects with the fingers; using a thick pencil, draw large circles on paper.
6. The patient should attempt to walk early and practice raising and swinging the affected leg while supporting himself; the walker can be used for support while doing this exercise. As a general rule, the patient may be gotten out of bed if there is stability at the hip and ankle and if his quadriceps muscle can function against gravity. Walking reeducation exercises should be graduated as progress is made. Posture and balance training is part of walking reeducation.
7. Pulley exercises are of great value in preventing adhesions and increasing range of motion. A small pulley is attached to a gooseneck pipe over the head of the bed; an ordinary clothesline is used for the rope and a piece of one-inch webbing forms the hand loop. Pulley therapy has an advantage over passive stretching exercises in that the patient, knowing his own pain threshold, will proceed more rapidly toward toleration of full range of motion.

Correction of Deformities

The most common residual complications of hemiplegia are shortening of the heel tendon (tendon of Achilles), resulting in plantar flexion of the foot and loss of shoulder movement — commonly referred to as frozen shoulder.

Shortened Heel Tendon

A shortened heel tendon must be corrected if the patient is ever to walk again. In most cases, passive stretching and the use of a short leg brace, with a 90 to 110° stop at the ankle to maintain the gains made by stretching, will correct this deformity. Shortened heel tendon is often accompanied by flexion contractures of the knee which can be corrected, in most instances, by passive stretching of the hamstring muscles.

Frozen Shoulder

A frozen shoulder is treated with passive movements, preceded by the application of heat, preferably moist, and massage. The objective is to increase the range of shoulder movement until the arm can be raised upward directly over the head. These passive exercises can be carried out by a physical therapist, nurse, member of the family, or the patient himself.

Pulley therapy is also helpful. The pulley is attached to the top of the door frame and the handle of a bucket filled with sand is fitted to each end of the pulley rope. Exercise with this apparatus promotes full flexion, abduction, and external rotation of the shoulder.

A frozen shoulder is painful, and the pain will continue until a full range of passive movement is possible.

Reeducation for Walking

With proper training, many hemiplegic patients can be taught to walk again. The degree to which normal gait can be restored depends on the amount of residual function retained by the quadriceps muscle on the affected side. The steps in retraining for ambulation are:

1. Get the patient out of bed and in the standing position as soon as possible. This will help prevent loss of the sense of balance and the development of disuse atrophy.
2. Fit a brace to the affected ankle to prevent plantar fixation and supination of the foot, which cause foot drop, and to give the patient confidence in weight bearing. A double-bar short leg brace with a stirrup attachment, a 90° ankle stop, and a supinator "T" strap is the most commonly prescribed type of brace.
3. Have the patient practice weight bearing on the involved leg, using two chairs or parallel bars for support.
4. Instruct the patient in the technic of reciprocal gait. This is the normal gait for walking and involves moving one leg and the opposite arm forward at the same time, then the other leg and its opposite arm.

   The hemiplegic patient walks without moving the affected arm which he abducts and rotates internally at the shoulder while flexing the elbow, wrist, and fingers. He also tends to circumduct the affected leg when trying to move it forward and often facilitates this circumduction by bending his trunk away from the affected side, thus tilting the pelvis upward on that side. Since these movements produce an awkward, slow, fatiguing gait, every effort should be made to get the patient to use the reciprocal gait technic.
5. Teach the patient to raise his foot from the floor by flexing his hip and knee, extending his affected leg forward at the knee, and then extending the hip until the foot touches the ground, heel first. The brace will prevent plantar flexion of the foot. This maneuver should be practiced faithfully, first within parallel bars and later with a crutch or cane for support.

With a brace, a cane, and persistent practice, most hemiplegic patients can learn to walk independently again.

Retraining the Arm and Hand

The reestablishment of arm movement in a hemiplegic patient should start with passive exercises to the shoulder and stretching. This helps to prevent flexion deformities at the elbow, wrist, fingers, and thumb, and should be carried out five or six times a day. As soon as some voluntary movement of the arm becomes possible, functional activities should be encouraged through occupational therapy activities.

Regaining General Body Control

The hemiplegic patient must be taught how to move in bed so that he can change his position from supine to prone and from supine to sitting. He must also learn to maintain his balance while sitting. He will need instruction in how to use his unaffected leg to move or raise his paralyzed leg and how to swing both legs laterally so as to bring them over the side of the bed preparatory to standing up.

The hemiplegic will also need instruction in how to get in and out of his wheelchair and how to propel it by using his unaffected arm and leg. Wheelchairs equipped with one-arm drive mechanism are available and are particularly useful for patients with unilateral paralysis.

The patient who can walk without the aid of a cane, brace, or crutch needs to learn how to cope with different floor surfaces indoors and different ground surfaces outdoors. He also must learn to stand up unassisted, to sit down, to climb stairs, to step up and down at curbings, and to cross the street.

Self-Care

It is not difficult for the hemiplegic patient to learn to perform such self-care activities as face-washing, teeth-brushing, hair-combing, and shaving, since these activites can readily be done with one hand. With the exception of cutting meat, eating can also be done with one hand only.

Bathing in a shower is usually recommended for these patients rather than tub bathing because getting in and out of a tub is often difficult for them.

Dressing is made easier by the use of clothing that opens down the front and does not have to be pulled on over the head. The paralyzed arm or leg should be clothed before the unaffected extremity. Coats and coatlike garments are more easily removed if grasped at the belt line rather than higher or lower than this.

As for the activites of daily living that are not directly concerned with self-care, many of them can be mastered by the hemiplegic if he has some guidance. It is not difficult, for instance, to use a telephone, open a desk drawer, or to open a lock with a key using only one hand. Writing may be a problem for the right-handed patient whose right side is paralyzed but, with practice, he will be able to write with his left hand. Also, there are many devices on the market that have been especially designed for these physically handicapped patients.

GUILLAIN-BARRE SYNDROME

Guillain-Barré syndrome is the term given to a condition seen in patients with viral encephalitis. It is characterized by the absence of fever, pain or tenderness in the muscles, motor weakness, and the abolition of motor reflexes.

Treatment

Treatment in the acute stage consists first of an evaluation of the patient's condition, and then utilization of the following modalities:

Range of motion exercises (passive)
Breathing exercises
Correct positioning in bed
Application of heat (hot packs or Hubbard tub)

Treatment during the later stages and during rehabilitation is based on an evaluation of the patient's needs and the results of tests of muscle strength. The modalities and activites employed include:

Range of motion exercises
Activites to develop functional skills
Reeducation of the affected muscle groups
Standing and balancing
Ambulation, including gait training
Functional activities to improve strength, dexterity, and range of motion of the upper extremities
Instruction in the performance of the activites of daily living

It is important that the patient not become fatigued in carrying out these therapeutic activities. His progress toward recovery will be slow, and the therapist should exercise caution and progress slowly in allowing the patient to engage in such activities as sitting up in bed or being out of bed, especially during the first few months of rehabilitation.

MULTIPLE SCLEROSIS

Multiple sclerosis is a highly complex, chronic, progressive, neurologic disease caused by changes in the white matter of the brain and spinal cord. The many symptoms vary in number and degree with each individual. One authority classifies multiple sclerosis as follows:

1. Acute (sudden onset)
2. Chronic remittent (characterized by extensive involvement and by exacerbations and remissions that are almost complete and last over a long period of time)
3. Chronic progressive (symptoms persist without any periods of remission)

Symptoms and Prognosis

The symptoms of multiple sclerosis usually develop slowly and gradually, although occasionally they may appear suddenly and be acute in nature. In most instances there is complete recovery from the first symptoms. This period of recovery, however, is actually a remission which varies in length from days to years

— there are reports of remissions that have lasted from 20 to 30 years. It has been noted that when the symptoms are the result of a large lesion that causes ataxia, paraplegia, or mental deterioration, they tend to become permanent.

The most common symptoms are diplopia, nystagmus, intention tremor, ataxia, weakness, slurred speech, and spasticity. When the cerebellum is involved, the patient often exhibits spasticity of one or both legs along with ataxia and tremor.

Emotional disturbances often accompany multiple sclerosis. The patient may be euphoric, depressed, or emotionally unstable, and experience personality changes and loss of memory.

The prognosis for multiple sclerosis is unfavorable. The course of the disease varies greatly, but survival is usually estimated at 5 to 20 years. The outlook for patients with a single or few symptoms is more favorable than for those with a combination of symptoms, as ordinarily occurs when the cerebellum is involved. Death is usually due to complications or conditions resulting from the patient's lowered resistance to infection.

Treatment

Goals and Objectives of Therapy

The physical therapist's objective for the patient with multiple sclerosis is to retrain him in ambulation, to help him maintain a high level of physical and mental activity, and to facilitate family management of the patient in the more advanced stages of his disease. Many patients are able to continue with their work, recreation, and social activities for a number of years after their disease has become established. The therapist should insist that the patient do as much as possible for himself for as long as he can. The use of assistive devices will often prolong his ability to do for himself. It is more psychologically sound for these patients to continue their activities within the limits imposed by their condition than for them to give up and assume the attitude of complete invalidism.

Corrective Therapy

The treatment of multiple sclerosis is largely corrective and necessarily individualized, with the type of therapy employed being directed toward the specific symptoms. One patient may display signs of hemiplegia, another may be ataxic and spastic, and still another will show a great variety of symptoms. In general, however, the approach to corrective therapy should anticipate progression of the disease and should include measures to prevent contractures, to regain or retain normal range of motion, to help the patient to utilize his remaining abilities to their fullest potential, and to retrain him in the activities of daily living.

One of the most important aspects of a rehabilitation program for patients with paralysis is the prevention of contractures. Exercise in the form of stretching helps to keep the paralyzed limb flexible so it can be moved through the complete range of motion. The patient should be encouraged to ambulate as long as possible and not to use bracing or ambulatory aids unless absolutely necessary.

Progressive resistive exercises are used to prevent muscle atrophy and to strengthen weak muscles so often seen in patients who have been on bed rest for a long time. The chief purpose of exercise for the ataxic patient is to develop muscle power, coordination, and endurance.

Since multiple sclerosis is a long-term disease, specialized training in the activities of daily living, or self-care, is a salient feature of any rehabilitation program; this can be provided by any physical or occupational therapist. Included in the training program are such activities as getting in and out of bed, getting into and out of a wheelchair, crutch walking, feeding oneself, dressing oneself, and so on, progressing through the various daily activities of a normal individual.

Patients with multiple sclerosis often complain of always being fatigued, and the therapist may wonder whether exercise is contraindicated. René Cailliet, who has worked with many patients with multiple sclerosis, has written that no medication is known to be specific in overcoming this fatigue and that, in his experience, only enforced and persistent exercise against resistance is effective in helping to overcome it.

MUSCULAR DYSTROPHY

Muscular dystrophy is an inborn abnormality of muscle characterized by dysfunction and eventual deterioration. Numerous types have been described but, regardless of type, the disease has an insidious onset, the chief symptoms being weakness, tightness and atrophy of muscles, and absence of deep tendon reflexes.

Tightness of muscles in the upper extremities occurs chiefly in the pronators of the forearm, the wrist and finger flexors, and the scapulohumeral flexors and adductors. Tightness in the lower extremities occurs early and affects chiefly the gastrocnemius, soleus, and hamstring muscles, the iliotibial band, and the hip flexors. Contractures also occur early and are severe, probably because the muscle itself is the site of the pathological lesion. Deformities caused by contractures are the principal reason for early loss of ambulation.

Treatment

The patient with muscular dystrophy should not be put on bed rest for minor illnesses but should be kept ambulatory if possible. The therapist should insist that the patient carry out all the activities he is capable of for as long as he can.

Exercises to increase flexibility of the muscles should be begun early. Breathing exercises are taught when indicated. Strengthening exercises are of unproven value, but unless the patient engages in active exercise he will become confined to a wheelchair sooner than is necessary. However, it is important that he not exercise to the point of fatigue. Massage may delay the development of contractures.

Braces and ambulatory aids are not used if the patient can manage without them. However, if contractures do not respond to physical therapy modalities, supportive splints or braces may be necessary and may defer the need for a wheelchair.

Since prolonged physical therapy is not warranted, the patient should be placed on a program of home care early, and then seen by a physical therapist on a regular check-up basis.

For this reason, it is essential that the patient receive early and adequate instruction in procedures for carrying out the activities of daily living.

PARKINSON'S DISEASE

Physical therapy can offer only temporary symptomatic improvement for patients with Parkinson's disease, but this is often of considerable benefit. Muscular rigidity can be lessened by active exercises. Under proper supervision and encouragement, some bedridden patients may be taught to walk again, improve their posture, and become relatively independent. Active exercises graded to tolerance are useful in combating disuse atrophy. In the event that limitation of motion has occurred and movement is painful, heat is of considerable help. Usually infrared radiation or hot fomentations, followed by sedative massage, are used. Hot tub baths are also beneficial in relaxing the patient and relieving some of the muscle spasm.

PERIPHERAL NERVE CONDITIONS

Peripheral nerve injuries and lesions may be caused by contusions, dislocation, fractures, wounds, or continuous pressure.

Not all loss of function seen in patients with peripheral nerve lesions is the result of defective conduction. Some may be the result of shock, local pain, swelling of tissues, fracture, dislocation, adhesions, ankylosis, contracture of opposing uninjured muscles, spasm, sclerosed fibrous tissue (as in ischemic paralysis), injury to tendons and muscles, or hysteria. Many times, an injury to a nerve produces paralysis of certain muscles, which leads to a characteristic deformity. The following simple tests and procedures for determining the location of a nerve lesion will give the physician an idea of the type of injury the patient has sustained and the treatment he requires.

A lesion of the *axillary (circumflex) nerve* produces a paralysis of the deltoid muscle. The patient is unable to abduct the arm and the weight of the unsupported arm often results in a subluxation of the head of the humerus and at least a marked stretching of the capsular ligament.

A lesion of the *median nerve* produces an inability to: (1) appose the thumb to the little finger, (2) abduct the thumb at right angles to the palm, (3) flex the index finger, as in making a fist or clasping the hands, and (4) flex the distal phalanx of the thumb.

A lesion of the *ulnar nerve* is easily recognized by the paralysis it produces: (1) clawing of the little and ring fingers, (2) inability to grasp objects between the thumb and forefinger (paralysis of the adductor pollicis muscle of the thumb), (3) inability to make a cone of the hand by approximating the tips of the fingers and thumb (paralysis of the interosseus muscles of the hand), and (4) inability to abduct the little finger.

A combined lesion of the *median* and *ulnar nerves* results in paralysis which, when complete, produces inability to perform any flexor movements of the fingers or hand. Loss of ability to abduct the little finger and to flex the distal phalanx of the index finger provides evidence of damage to both nerves at a location above the wrist and midforearm.

A lesion of the *radial nerve* may be identified by extending the wrist and proximal phalanges of the fingers and thumb in a plane with the palm and then bringing the palms together (palm to palm test); the only conspicuous defect seen is in the angle between the hand and forearm. When the palms are separated the affected hand drops at the wrist.

A lesion of the *peroneal nerve* results in drop foot and a complete paralysis of the anterior and lateral muscles of the leg, which causes a foot deformity (talipes varus). The os calcis is raised considerably because there is no opposing action by the gastrocnemius muscle. The peroneal group of muscles and the extensors attached to the inner side of the foot are also paralyzed, causing flatfoot from the lack of support to the arches. A serious disability in walking develops because of the overaction necessary to keep the toes from scraping the ground.

A lesion of the *tibial nerve* results in deformities that are practically the opposite of those resulting from injuries to the peroneal nerve. The lack of opposing action by the peroneal muscles allows the foot to be pulled into dorsiflexion; the os-calcis is directed downward instead of backward; the foot tends to assume the valgus position; and the longitudinal arch flattens because of the paralysis of the tibialis posterior and the small muscles of the foot.

A lesion of the *femoral nerve* is commonly accompanied by injuries to pelvic vessels and viscera. The quadriceps femoris, sartorius, and pectineus muscles are all paralyzed. The patient is unable to stand upon his leg unless the knee and leg are in extreme extension. The knee joint soon becomes unstable and may suddenly flex, causing the patient to fall. When walking, the patient usually bends forward and places his hand on his thigh to keep the knee and leg securely extended. The tensor fasciae latae muscle may act to hold the joint in fixed extension, and then the patient assumes a swinging gait.

In addition to the tests for locating the site of a lesion of a peripheral nerve, there are many other diagnostic procedures and tests available, such as electromyography, chronaxy, dermometry, sign of Tinel, reactions to galvanic and faradic current, and Minor's sweat test. Since special training and equipment are needed to perform these tests, the patient is usually referred to a neurologist.

Treatment

Treatment for peripheral nerve conditions involves the use of several physical therapy modalities. The objectives of the therapist differ somewhat in the various conditions. When a primary suture is possible, or when the patient is brought in for treatment soon after an injury that does not require an operation, the aim is to prevent deformities and to restore function. Operative procedures of suture and the liberation of the nerve from adhesions will not serve to restore function, but only make it possible for the nerve to regenerate.

Some of the most common physical therapy modalities employed include:

1. Splinting: to prevent overstretching of paralyzed or weak muscles

2. Massage: to improve the nutrition of affected parts, prevent adhesions of scars and fibrosis, and conserve the bulk of the muscle
3. Passive movement: to prevent deformity from shortening and fibrosis or from ankylosis of joints
4. Active exercise: to conserve the unparalyzed muscles, stimulate circulation, and educate synergistic muscles to assume the function of paralyzed muscles
5. Electrotherapy: to conserve vitality, prevent complete atony, and increase contractility of paralyzed muscles
6. Heat: to increase circulation and to help and facilitate other forms of treatment

The most desirable method of providing heat is the whirlpool bath at temperatures from 100° to 105°F for 30 minutes. Under the combined action of heat and gentle massage, the clammy, tender limb becomes warm, red, free from pain, and ready for any other type of treatment.

Excessive heat or diathermy is not safe to use in scar lesions that are associated with peripheral nerve lesions; the disturbance in sensory reception and lack of normal collateral circulation may cause excessive heat to result in slow-healing burns.

Occupational therapy should play a big part in the patient's regimen.

Results of treatments for this pathological condition are rather slow, and the patient should be told this to prevent discouragement.

POLYNEURITIS

Polyneuritis (multiple peripheral neuritis) is a condition in which there is inflammation of many nerves at once. It is characterized by degeneration of the involved nerves, with resulting impairment or loss of conduction along the nerve fibers, and varying degrees of motor, sensory, and reflex impairment. Although the symptoms are the same for all types of polyneuritis, the condition is usually classified according to its cause:

Nutritional deficiency (alcoholic neuritis is the most common type in this group)

Chemicals and drugs (arsenic, lead, sulfonamides, barbital, carbon dioxide)

Certain pathological conditions (pellagra, pernicious anemia, beriberi, diabetes)

Infections

Symptoms

The symptoms of polyneuritis may be divided into two groups — sensory and motor. The chief sensory symptom is pain, in varying degrees.

Motor disturbances, the area of most interest to the physical therapist, vary from mild weakness to total paralysis. The paralysis in this disease is of the flaccid type and there is marked atrophy of the involved muscles. Foot drop is a common symptom in alcoholic neuritis, and ataxia is noted when the patient attempts to stand; weakness and ataxia are the two most marked physical symptoms. The symptoms may last for days, months, or years, depending on the amount of damage the nerves have received.

When the condition is caused by a poison such as arsenic, the patient may become quadriplegic and practically all muscle groups will be involved; the distal portions of the limbs will be more involved than the proximal portions.

Treatment

The physical therapist's objective for the patient with polyneuritis is to help restore him to good physical condition and to make it possible for him to walk, with or without aids. The therapist's success will depend, of course, on the amount of nerve damage the patient has sustained.

The modalities employed will be determined by the physical symptoms displayed by the patient. The primary symptom in alcoholic neuritis ranges from weakness to ataxia and paralysis. Any exercise program for these patients should include progressive resistive exercises for strengthening the weakened muscles, and exercises to improve coordination.

The patient who suffers from poisoning by a drug, such as arsenic, is usually totally paralyzed and his muscles will be atrophied. In these cases the therapist tries to prevent contractures; assistive exercises are an important modality.

Prognosis

The prognosis in polyneuritis varies with the amount of damage the nerve has received. Recovery is usually slow. Patients with alcoholic neuritis often recover sufficiently to allow them to walk with the aid of a cane. In cases of severe poisoning, many months of therapy may be required before recovery occurs, and then the outcome depends on whether proper preventive measures were taken against contractures and muscle atrophy.

PROTRUSION OF INTERVERTEBRAL DISK

During the period of diagnostic study to determine the necessity for operation, physical therapy can be of much help in most cases of suspected protrusion of an intervertebral disk. Measures may include rest on a firm mattress, traction to the legs or head or both, and the use of heat and sedative massage at the painful areas. Diathermy (which must be very mild and of short duration) or infrared radiation may be used, preferably the latter. Frequently, the symptoms will be relieved by such treatments within a few weeks. Then gradual mobilization is started and various exercises for muscles in the abdominal, gluteal, and lumbar regions are given. Patients should be taught how to prevent excessive back strain when stooping and sitting down, and during other bodily movements.

RADICULITIS

Radiculitis is a neurologic condition caused by irritation of the spinal nerve roots, and manifested by pain and by alterations in perception of sensation or in muscle function. The syndrome consists of restricted mobility of the spine, root pain, and root sensory alterations, all of which are produced or aggravated by movement. Radiculitis may involve various parts of the body including the arms, trunk, thorax, and lower limbs. Cervical involvement is associated with headache and painful neck, shoulders, and arms.

It is important that the patient rest in bed and on a hard mattress. Cervical traction is a very important part of the treatment (see pp. 64–65 for method of application of cervical traction). Mild heat and very mild massage may also be useful.

SCALENUS ANTICUS SYNDROME

Scalenus anticus syndrome is the term used to describe the neurologic disorder that is characterized by pain over the shoulder often extending down the arm to the forearm and fingers or radiating up the back of the neck. The referred pain may follow the course of any of the cervical or brachial nerves, especially the fourth, fifth, and sixth cervical, and is usually felt in the supraspinatus and trapezius muscles and in the occipital region. Palpation usually reveals areas of tenderness and areas of thickening along the spinal ligaments. Symptoms are made worse by work and exercise. Cramps in the fingers and coldness, numbness, and tingling of the hand are common symptoms.

Treatment

Conservative therapeutic treatment includes keeping the arm elevated above the shoulder with the hand behind the head. Such elevation of the arm and shoulder girdle displaces the brachial plexus upward and out of the scalenus triangle and thus relieves tension upon the nervous and vascular structures.

Heat may be applied over the region of the scalenus muscle.

Good results have been obtained by correction of the patient's posture.

Other methods of obtaining relief include elevating the shoulder by means of a sling or by holding the hand across the chest inside a buttoned shirt or coat, eliminating work that aggravates the symptoms, and sleeping with the arm elevated over the head (this relaxes the squeezing mechanism that compresses the brachial plexus and causes pain).

SCIATICA

Three main forms of sciatica are distinguished:

1. Subacute and chronic sciatica associated with rheumatism and arthritis
2. True neuritic sciatica
3. Sciatica associated with prolapse of an intervertebral disk

Treatment

During the acute stage, the patient should rest in bed on a firm mattess with a fracture board between the mattress and spring. The affected leg may be partially flexed by placing a pillow under the knee and a small, firm pillow under the lumbar area. Heat may be applied to the lower gluteal region and lower back but should be discontinued if it causes an increase in pain. Diathermy may be used, but it should be of low intensity. Ultrasound therapy has proved beneficial.

After the acute pain has subsided, massage and postural exercises are begun while the patient is still on bed rest, and he is taught how to breathe correctly. Before he is allowed up he should be fitted with a lower back support and taught to maintain his improved posture. If one leg is shorter than the other, a heel lift may be required.

TABES DORSALIS

In tabes dorsalis one of the most troublesome symptoms is ataxia, the impairment of muscular coordination. By means of precision exercises it is possible to restore some of this impaired coordination and to reeducate the patient in various movements. This is purely symptomatic treatment, exerting no influence upon the lesions or the course of the disease except enabling the patient to help himself. These special (Frenkel) exercises are of two kinds, one for bedridden and one for ambulatory patients.

Exercises for Bedridden Patients

The patient is taught to flex, abduct, adduct, and extend each leg separately and both legs simultaneously. To exercise the knees and hips, the patient should place the heel of one foot on the knee of the opposite leg and then pass it slowly down the tibia toward the ankle.

These exercises should be carried out with the eyes open and closed. They may be repeated twice daily as long as the patient's condition requires.

Exercises for Ambulatory Patients

1. The patient is placed with his back to a chair, with his heels together, and then lowers himself slowly into the chair and rises again. Crutches or canes should not be used. It may be necessary at first for an attendant to support the patient.
2. One leg is placed in front of the other at the distance of an ordinary walking step, then returned accurately to the original position. The patient may, if necessary, support himself with a cane during this exercise.
3. The patient walks several steps, slowly and with precision.
4. In the standing position, the patient places one foot in front of the other. With his hands across his chest, he flexes his knees and then slowly raises himself.
5. Exercise 2 may be repeated and extended so that the patient places one foot *behind* the other. This reeducates his sense of balance.
6. With the feet together, the patient stands alone with his hands on his hips.
7. With the feet separated in a normal standing position, and without a cane, the patient performs various actions with his hands and arms.

These exercises may be lengthened and enlarged as the patient develops his coordination. They are, of course, also valuable in the treatment of flaccid paraplegia.

19
PERIPHERAL VASCULAR DISORDERS

TREATMENT

Heat

Heat is a powerful vasodilator which acts directly upon the blood vessels. Heat in sufficient doses increases the temperature of the blood. Applied to any part of the body, heat increases the local tissue temperature and local tissue metabolism; it produces direct local hyperemia and reflex vasodilatation in distant parts of the body surface. In severe organic vascular obstruction with inadequate collateral circulation, the possible degree of vasodilatation and improved blood flow may not equal the greater need for blood. Heat application then increases ischemia, resulting in pain and discoloration. In the presence of insufficient blood flow, the dissipation of externally applied heat is diminished and the danger of burn is great. Direct heat application to a limb with organic vascular obstruction is, therefore, indicated if there is a fair circulatory reserve. In advanced cases, heat should be used only under most careful supervision. If the patient complains of increased pain, heat treatment should be stopped immediately.

In peripheral vascular disease, circulation of the extremities should be increased by warming the patient's trunk and thighs or opposite normal extremities (reflex action). Electric heating pads and hot-water bottles should not be applied directly to the affected extremities. Thermostatically controlled heating is the safest. Hot soaks may be used in the treatment of gangrene and ulcers, but the water should never be warmer than 102° to 105°F. Contrast baths are recommended as a home treatment, especially for the symptoms of intermittent claudication and frostbite. Cold has also been recently recommended to safeguard against or minimize gangrene resulting from arterial occlusion.

An infrared or radiant lamp is very satisfactory, since heat from such a source does not penetrate deeply. It should be used for 30 minutes twice a day. Short-wave diathermy may be used with caution for intermittent claudication; it should be administered in very low dosage for 30 minutes.

Iontophoresis

Iontophoresis with a vasodilating drug (Mecholyl) is being employed in certain types of peripheral vascular disease. Good results have been reported in Raynaud's disease and scleroderma. Chronic ulcers, associated either with varicose veins or with occlusion following phlebitis, seem to respond very well to this treatment.

Rhythmic Constriction (Intermittent Venous Occlusion)

A constrictor produced by an inflatable cuff will bring about increased blood flow by active dilation of the arterioles of the compressed extremity. It is used in acute vascular occlusion and vascular diseases with major involvement of the large vessels. The use of a rhythmic constrictor is contraindicated in cases of thrombophlebitis, cellulitis, or lymphangitis (acute or subacute), extensive destruction of the arteriolar or capillary vessels, advanced thromboangiitis obliterans and capillary stasis, advanced arteriosclerosis with capillary stasis, and venous thrombosis.

Buerger-Allen Exercise

In addition to the various other treatments used for peripheral circulatory disturbances, it is helpful to increase the collateral circulation by inducing reactionary hyperemia. This may best be accomplished by having the patient perform the Buerger-Allen exercise, shown in the drawings below (reprinted with permission of the publisher from *Peripheral Circulatory*

Stimulation by Physical Means, copyright 1971 by Scicom, Inc.). This exercise is divided into the following three stages:

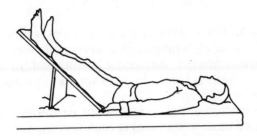

Stage 1. The patient lies on his back, with a watch in sight, rests his legs on an inclined plane that is raised to an angle of 45°, and keeps them raised until his feet are thoroughly blanched. This requires 2 minutes, as a rule.

Stage 2. The patient sits with his legs hanging over the edge of the bed and puts his feet and toes through a series of motions. He flexes his ankles downward, and then upward; rocks his feet inward (flexing the tibial muscles), and then outward (flexing the fibular muscles); spreads his toes and then closes them. As he performs these movements, his feet become flushed; the entire foot to the tips of the toes should be a strong pink color. This usually requires from 1 to 3 minutes. If the toes become cyanotic or painful, the feet should be elevated at once.

Stage 3. For 5 minutes the patient lies supine in bed with his legs horizontal, wrapped in a woolen blanket and warmed by a hot-water bottle or an electric heating pad. In this way, the reactionary flush achieved by the exercises in stages 1 and 2 is maintained.

The duration of the cycle is about 10 minutes. The exercise is performed three to six times at each session, and the session is repeated two to four times a day.

Treatment for Thromboangiitis Obliterans

Preserve natural warmth of the extremities by woolen socks and woolen underwear.

Hot baths, not over 105°F, with the water level up to the hips for 10-minute periods just before retiring, are very effective in the production of vasodilatation of the lower extremities. Hot baths should also be taken immediately following postural exercises.

Short wave diathermy at low temperature (very mild heat) for 20 minutes, three times a week, may be helpful.

Treatment for Raynaud's Disease

Avoidance of exposure to cold is very important.

A daily hot bath, not over 105°F, is valuable. The bath is most effective if taken before retiring.

Iontophoresis with Mecholyl may be effective.

20
POSTMASTECTOMY EDEMA

Significant lymphedema of the arm develops in one-third to one-half of the patients who undergo radical mastectomy. The arm may increase as much as 3 centimeters over its preoperative diameter, and the condition may occur at any time. Usually, however, it occurs during the first year after surgery.

The swollen arm is not only a cosmetic insult to a woman who has undergone breast removal but it sometimes becomes subject to recurring cellulitis, and occasionally progresses to sarcoma.

TREATMENT

Physical therapy is being using increasingly in the treatment of postmastectomy lymphedema. Currently the most commonly used modality is intermittent compression with pressure gradient fabric supports. Results have been fair to good. This treatment results in pronounced reduction of edema and relief of pain. In many cases, there is an attendant psychological lift as edema is reduced and the patient's arm returns to normal size.

The first step in the treatment program consists of reducing the edema in the extremity by gentle, controlled pneumatic massage. When the amount of fluid in the tissues has been reduced so that the arm approaches normal size, exclusive pressure gradient fabric supports are applied. This kind of support provides a resilient counteraction against the tissues, lymphatic system, and venous vessels to offset the internal hydrostatic pressures. Because of the gradient pressure, every muscle movement assists in the upward movement of venous and lymphatic fluids. Thus, this treatment produces a physiological change in the fluid dynamics of the extremity by preventing venous lymphatic stasis.

The treatment is repeated two to three times weekly. The number of treatments needed depends on the patient's condition when treatment started. Usually, after approximately two weeks the patient is measured for gradient support.

After the edema has been satisfactorily reduced, the patient may elect to discontinue the treatments, but she is warned to continue wearing the support.

Swelling may recur, but usually a few treatments will reduce the edema. Some patients who have had lymphedema following mastectomy elect to return to a clinic, at regular intervals, for a treatment with the intermittent pressure unit in order to prevent a recurrence of the condition.

21
THORACIC AND RESPIRATORY CONDITIONS

Many hospitals have separate inhalation therapy departments with specially trained therapists in attendance. Therefore, only a brief outline of general information about physical therapy procedures used in respiratory and thoracic conditions will be given here. However, thoracic surgeons and general practitioners sometimes refer patients who have certain respiratory conditions to the physical therapy department for selected exercises, primarily breathing exercises, and these will be described.

Several factors influence the rate and depth of breathing, including the amount of oxygen and carbon dioxide in the blood. These factors are all coordinated in the respiratory center, a small group of cells at the base of the brain that controls and activates the nerves that supply the muscles used in breathing. Whenever the patient is unable to take in and expel the normal amount of air from the lungs, the balance between oxygen and carbon dioxide in the lungs and in the bloodstream is altered. This alteration is reflected in the action of the respiratory center and, consequently, in the way one breathes.

Physical therapy has much to offer to patients with respiratory conditions such as emphysema, asthma, or bronchitis. Breathing becomes difficult for these individuals because there is a narrowing of some segment in the respiratory tree and this interferes with the flow of air both into and out of the lungs. Breathing exercises, correctly and consistently done, will help to improve the patient's breathing by strengthening the diaphragm as well as the chest and back muscles used in breathing. The objective of therapy is to assist the patient to breathe more comfortably and efficiently, with less effort, all of the time. A few minutes should be set aside each day to run through the exercises described below. Some patients find it

most helpful to do their first exercises of the day immediatel
upon awakening in the morning.

Although several physical therapy modalities are employee
in treating patients with respiratory or thoracic conditions
breathing exercises are the most commonly used and, amon
these, exercises that strengthen the diaphragm and thu
promote correct, diaphragmatic breathing, are perhaps th
most basic. But other muscles are also used in breathing –
certain abdominal muscles, the lateral chest muscles, and som
of the back muscles, for example — and they too can b
strengthened by specific exercises.

BREATHING EXERCISES

Exercise to Correct Posture

It may be necessary to correct the patient's posture before h
can receive the maximum benefit from some of the breathing
exercises. Until he is fully aware of his posture, it is well for him
to perform the following exercise while standing before a
mirror.

With his shoulders erect and his chest thrust forward, he
breathes in slowly through the nose, gradually increasing the
amount of air he inhales. Then he expels the air slowly while
keeping his chin up and maintaining correct posture.

Exercises to Strengthen the Diaphragm and
Promote Diaphragmatic Breathing

The diaphragm is a sheet of muscle that forms a movable
partition between the chest and abdominal cavities. At rest, the
diaphragm is normally curved upward in a low dome. When it
is contracted or tightened by effort, it flattens out and makes
the chest cavity larger, and when it is relaxed it moves upward
and makes the chest cavity smaller and thus helps to move air in
and out of the lungs. This muscle works in coordination with
the chest muscles. In reality, it does most of the work. When
the lungs are overly full, as occurs in emphysema, the

diaphragm flattens out and remains fixed in the downward position, and thus does not give the patient all the breathing help it should. In fact, with the exception of singers and athletes, many healthy people rarely get as much help in breathing from the diaphragm as they could.

Many of the exercises for strengthening the diaphragm do so by the direct effect of the exercise on the diaphragm itself and by also strengthening its muscle attachments.

In one of the more simple exercises a sandbag weighing between 5 and 15 pounds is placed on the upper abdomen while the patient lies flat on the bed. As he breathes in, the diaphragm will contract and descend, making the upper abdomen rise; as he exhales, the diaphragm will relax and the abdomen falls. This exercise may be done in conjunction with the arm-lift exercise described later. In this exercise, as the patient elevates his arms and inhales, the sandbag will rise, and as he exhales while bringing his arms down, the sandbag will be brought closer to the spinal column. This exercise should be done for 10 to 15 minutes, three times a day.

Belly Breathing Exercises

One important group of exercises, sometimes called belly breathing exercises, if performed correctly and consistently, will result in easier breathing as the diaphragm and other breathing muscles become stronger and correct breathing becomes a healthful habit.

The patient lies on a firm, flat surface, without a pillow, his knees drawn up and his back flat on the surface. He places one hand over his ribs and one over his abdomen with the thumb just below the navel. As he breathes in, he allows the abdomen to protrude as far as it will go while the chest remains stationary. He then exhales slowly through pursed lips while pressing his abdomen firmly inward and upward while the chest still remains at rest. If he can feel his abdomen protrude as he inhales, he is breathing correctly. The patient can continue the exercise by placing both hands on the abdomen just below the navel with the fingertips touching, inhaling deeply through the

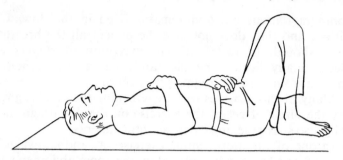

Figure 6. Basic position for belly breathing exercise. (Drawing reprinted by permission from *What You Can Do about Your Breathing* [American Lung Association, 1975]. The exercise was developed by Albert Haas, M.D., Department of Rehabilitation, New York University Medical Center.)

nose for one or two seconds, and exhaling through the mouth for five seconds while pressing with his hands to help expel the air from the bases of the lungs.

A similar exercise can be performed while sitting in a chair. The patient places both hands on his chest with the little fingers resting on the lowest ribs. As he exhales slowly through the mouth, he squeezes the ribs to help expel air from the lower part of the lungs. He may repeat this 8 to 12 times, resting when necessary.

Another belly breathing exercise that will help the patient to mark his progress in learning to breathe correctly involves only one exhalation at a time. A lighted candle is placed on a table in front of him and he is instructed to blow it out with one breath. Then, still breathing correctly, he moves the candle farther away and again blows it out with one breath. This procedure is repeated and a record is kept of the distance at which the flame can still be extinguished with one breath.

The patient can also measure his progress by placing a Ping-Pong ball on a large level table and measuring the distance he can blow the ball with one breath. Another trick with a Ping-Pong ball is to attach the ball to about 2 feet of string that is fastened to the top of a door frame with Scotch-tape. Making

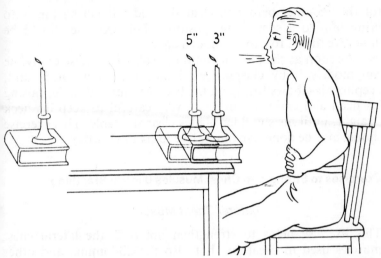

Figure 7. A breathing exercise that can also be used to test the patient's progress in learning diaphragmatic breathing. (Drawing reprinted by permission from *What You Can Do about Your Breathing* [American Lung Association, 1975]. The exercise was developed by Albert Haas, M.D., Department of Rehabilitation, New York University Medical Center.)

sure that the ball is still before he starts, the patient blows it to see how long he can keep it propelled away from himself before he must inhale. He should keep track of the time and try to increase the time he can cause the ball to remain propelled away from himself. Ordinarily it should not be necessary to continue these exercises for over 5 minutes at a time, but they should be repeated at least 5 times a day.

**Exercise to Strengthen Abdominal Muscles
Used in Breathing**

This exercise is performed with the patient lying on his back with his knees flexed and his feet placed firmly on the mattress. While keeping his neck in a straight line with his head and shoulders, his arms at his sides, and without using his elbows for assistance, he raises the upper part of his trunk just enough for the shoulder blades to clear the bed but not so far as to bring him to a semisitting position. This exercise should be done five times, five to six times a day.

As soon as the patient can do the above exercise easily, he can modify it by clasping his hands behind his neck and, keeping his elbows firmly on the bed or treatment table, raising his head and chest, again being very careful to keep his neck straight, until his shoulder blades clear the table. This exercise should also be done five times, five to six times a day.

Exercises to Strengthen Chest Muscles Used in Breathing

Lateral Chest Muscles

This exercise helps to strengthen not only the lateral chest muscles used in breathing but also the abdominal and other chest muscles. The patient lies flat on the bed, his knees flexed and his feet firmly placed on the mattress, and raises his trunk while twisting it either to the right or left. He may hold his hands behind his head or raise them forward to the right or left. The exercise should be repeated five times with the patient twisting to the right and five times with him twisting to the left.

Arm-Lift Exercise

This exercise can be done in the standing position or when lying down. It helps to increase the exchange of air in the lungs.

In the standing position the patient breathes in slowly through the nose while, at the same time, raising his arms forward and upward until they are fully extended over his head. He will then have taken in as much air as he can. Then he slowly lowers his arms while exhaling slowly, using one-third more time than he did to inhale. These movements should be done rhythmically with both arms being moved slowly and evenly and not jerked up and down, and the patient should not use force when exhaling. It is most important that the arms be brought up and lowered toward the front and not to the sides, and that the patient remain relaxed, not tense, during the exercise.

At first, it is important for the therapist to observe the patient to make sure that he lifts the lowermost part of the rib cage when he inhales and raises the rib cage when he exhales. It may be helpful for the patient to stand before a mirror as he does this exercise so he can see whether he is performing it correctly.

The arm-lift exercise is repeated five times every 2 to 3 hours during the day. For children, the exercise is repeated five times before and after meals, making a total of six exercise periods during the day. The number of breaths should not be increased beyond the number prescribed.

If the patient cannot perform the exercise in the standing position, he may remain in bed or on a firm cot or the floor. He should raise his arms as far over his head as possible, and do the exercise as described above, five or six times a day.

Hand-clapping Exercises

For the hand-clapping exercise, the patient stands erect and, while maintaining good posture, brings his hands forward and claps them, then throws his arms backward as far as he can while keeping them at shoulder height. He then brings the arms forward and repeats the procedure. There should be a definite, steady rhythm to the movements, which should be neither fast nor slow.

Hand-clapping exercises are performed ten times twice daily.

Exercise to Strengthen Back Muscles Used in Breathing

The use of exercise pulleys will help strengthen the muscles of the back that are used in breathing. A substitute can easily be arranged for use at home by using buckets of sand for weights, a window sash cord, and pulleys that can be purchased at any hardware store.

The patient uses his arms alternately to lift the weights, one arm at a time. The exercise is repeated as ordered by the physician.

Exercises to Assist Expiration

The Belt-pressure Exercise

A wide belt is placed over the patient's lower ribs just above the waistline. During expiration, either the patient or an assistant pulls on the two ends of the belt. This will help to squeeze air out of the lungs.

Pursed-lip Exercise

In pursed-lip breathing, the lips are "pursed" as in kissing, and the air is gently exhaled through the small opening between the lips. This improves the evenness of distribution of air and oxygen in the lungs, and helps keep the air tubes from narrowing and collapsing during expiration, which is the most difficult phase of respiration.

The patient should take a deep breath. Then he should exhale slowly, through pursed lips, making a soft blowing sound, and continue exhaling as long as he can — for at least twice as long as it took him to inhale. It may be helpful to use a timer for this exercise, allowing, for example, three half-second beats for breathing in and six beats for breathing out.

This exercise should be carried out five times every five minutes until it has been done 25 times, and the procedure repeated three times a day or as often as recommended by the physician.

EMPHYSEMA

Emphysema is a fairly common lung condition characterized by abnormal enlargement of the alveolar spaces in the lungs and destructive changes in the alveolar walls, which result in the collection of air in the interstices of the connective tissue and the intra-alveolar tissue of the lungs. These changes often cause an impairment in a most vital aspect of breathing — that is, the ability of the lungs to exchange air efficiently. Emphysema may occur at any age, and is most commonly seen in heavy smokers.

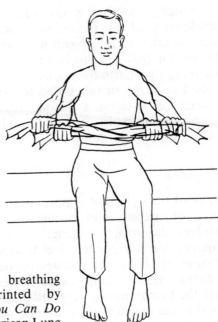

Figure 8. Belt-pressure breathing exercise. (Drawing reprinted by permission from *What You Can Do about Your Breathing* [American Lung Association, 1975]. The exercise was developed by Albert Haas, M.D., Department of Rehabilitation, New York University Medical Center.)

Figure 9. Pursed-lip breathing exercise. (Drawing reprinted by permission from *What You Can Do about Your Breathing*. [American Lung Association, 1975]. The exercise was developed by Albert Haas, M.D., Department of Rehabilitation, New York University Medical Center.)

Emphysema has many causes. It may be due to a hereditary weakness in the lung tissue, which leads to repeated overdistention of the alveoli with air, and this may so weaken the alveoli that distention becomes a permanent condition. Anything that partially blocks a bronchus may also cause the disease since the air tubes tend to widen during inhalation and air can get in around the blockage, but the tubes become narrow during expiration and thus all of the inhaled air cannot get out during expiration.

Symptoms

Many of the signs and symptoms of emphysema are similar to those of asthma and bronchitis, but emphysema usually involves the greatest restriction of breathing and therefore requires the most extensive treatment. Perhaps the most obvious sign is the barrel-shaped appearance of the thorax; this is characteristic of emphysema. Careful observation will show that the thorax moves very little during breathing; it remains fixed in the position of expiration. Chest expansion is reduced from the usual 3 or 4 inches to 1 or 1½ inches; the ribs are raised; and the sternum is thrust forward, resulting in an increase in the anterior-posterior diameter of the chest. The patient is cyanotic and dyspneic and finds it difficult to do breathing exercises because he becomes "out of breath."

Treatment

The aim of physical therapy in the treatment of emphysema is to help the patient to breathe more efficiently without the use of a nebulizer or other breathing device. Properly done exercises to strengthen muscles will help to bring more oxygen into his lungs and thus reduce his dyspnea, and postural drainage will help to remove obstructions in the bronchial tubes.

Exercises

Exercises that are helpful in the treatment of emphysema include the arm-lift breathing exercise, exercises to increase the strength of abdominal muscles and of lateral chest muscles used in breathing, hand-clapping, and exercises to correct posture, all of which are described earlier in this chapter.

Postural Drainage

Emphysema is one of the several chest conditions in which the patient cannot readily bring up mucus and secretions from the lower parts of the lungs by coughing. Both the accumulation of secretions and the fact that they may become infected will cause further obstruction in the air passages. Postural drainage is an easily performed procedure that will help to empty the lower parts of the lungs and air tubes by utilizing the force of gravity. The therapist can be most helpful to the patient in assisting him in getting into and out of the positions required for postural drainage.

One of the easiest postural drainage positions for the patient to achieve is to lie on his abdomen over two or three pillows, thus raising the bases of his lungs higher than his shoulders. He rests his head on his folded arms and turns his face alternately to the right and left. He may alter this position by placing his right arm on the right side of the bed and allowing the left arm to hang down over the side of the bed when he turns his face to the right; the position of the arms is reversed when he turns his face to the left. This position should be assumed for at least 15 to 20 minutes the first thing in the morning and again before retiring.

Another simple position for postural drainage is the head-down position, which aids both in the removal of secretions and in inspiration. It consists simply of elevating the foot of the bed about 14 inches; the patient may lie on his back or face down. This will cause the weight of the abdominal contents to push the diaphragm up, thus forcing out residual air along with mucus and secretions. At first, this position should be assumed for 15 to 20 minutes, four times a day. Later, the time is extended every week as directed by the physician. Many people learn to sleep all night in this position. The patient may also practice this exercise by leaning over the side of the bed or a couch for 15 to 20 minutes four times a day.

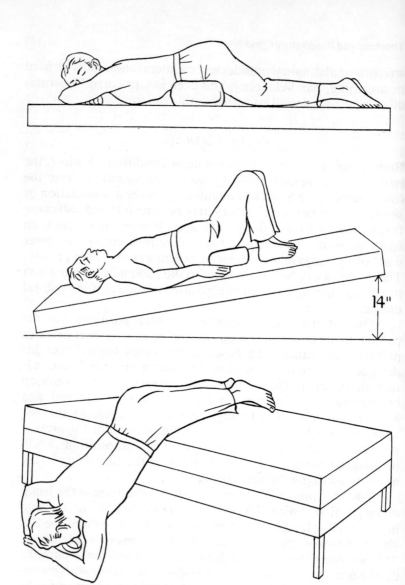

Figure 10. Three positions for postural drainage. (Drawings reprinted by permission from *What You Can Do about Your Breathing* [American Lung Association, 1975]. The exercise was developed by Albert Haas, M.D., Department of Rehabilitation, New York University Medical Center.)

A third lying-down position that can be used to induce postural drainage requires the patient to lie crosswise on the bed with his hips kept firmly on the surface of the bed and the upper part of his body extended over the side of the bed with the head down and resting on his hands, which are placed on the floor. He turns his torso to the right for a few minutes and then to the left, while an assistant holds his legs so that the lower part of his body remains flat on the bed. Then, while face down, he coughs in a series of gentle throat-clearing coughs, holding his breath for a few minutes after each cough, and then breathing in gently. This will bring mucus and secretions up from the deeper parts of the lungs into the larger air passages. This exercise should be done for 20 minutes four times a day. The patient can do two things to make the head-down position more effective: (1) keep his coughs gentle to prevent pulling phlegm back into the smaller passages of the deeper parts of the lungs during the next inhalation, and (2) tap the front of his chest with the fingertips of both hands in a regular pattern starting at the bottom and proceding upward toward the throat and then back down the chest, while an assistant taps the back in the same pattern; this will loosen the phlegm and can be done both during and after the exercise.

ASTHMA

Asthma is characterized by recurrent attacks of dyspnea during which expiration is particularly labored. These attacks are the result of spasm of the smooth muscle of the bronchi, swelling of the mucous lining, and increased secretion of mucus. The spasm causes partial obstruction of the bronchi and, consequently, extreme difficulty in expiration. Inspiration is not so difficult because, as the chest expands, the smaller bronchi increase in diameter and the obstruction is at least partially overcome. But as the intrapleural pressure rises on expiration, the lungs recoil, the bronchi decrease in diameter, and the obstruction tends to be increased. Since air can be drawn in but not expelled, the alveoli become increasingly distended and dyspnea and cyanosis result. Once the spasm

ceases, mucus is coughed up, the muscular walls of the bronch
relax, and breathing becomes normal. These attacks occur mos
frequently in children but may also occur in older persons.

Asthma is thought to be due to an allergy to some
otherwise harmless substance.

Symptoms

The symptoms of asthma are as described above. They are
usually temporary and disappear when the causative allergen is
discovered and the patient can be desensitized to it. No
permanent damage is done by the attacks, but they will recur
again and again until the allergen is discovered and steps taken
to counteract it. But even without such treatment, some
patients may be free of symptoms for long periods of time.

Treatment

In most cases of asthma the ability to use the diaphragm in
breathing and to expand the basal areas of the lungs is lost. In
addition, the chest is often tense and the neck muscles in
vigorous action, making it almost impossible to practice
diaphragmatic breathing. Therefore the patient has to be taught
how to relax and keep the upper thorax still and to use the
diaphragm in breathing (see page 170). The objective in all
exercises is to help the patient empty the lungs.

It is important to help the patient gain a longer expiration
time so that emphysematous changes do not occur in the lungs.
The first step is to attempt to reduce the size of the thorax
during expiration. Once this is mastered, a longer expiration
time can be gained by pressing on the thorax with the hands
during expiration.

Exercises which can be given and supervised by any well-
trained physical therapist include: exercises for strengthening
the diaphragm, the lateral costal muscles, and the back and
abdominal muscles used in breathing; exercises to improve the
posture; hand-clapping; arm-lift exercises; the belt-pressure
exercise; and pursed-lip breathing.

BRONCHITIS, CHRONIC

Chronic bronchitis is a respiratory condition characterized by chronic inflammation of the lining of the larger and medium-sized bronchi, usually occurring as a result of infection. It is most common in middle-aged and elderly people, especially those living in industrial areas or in cold, damp climates, and those with low resistance. It may also be caused by irritation from some chemicals, gases, dust, and smoke.

Treatment

The chief aim in the treatment of chronic bronchitis is to increase the patient's intake of oxygen. It is also important to raise the resistance of the bronchial tree to infection.

The various exercises utilized in the treatment of emphysema and asthma are also used in treating chronic bronchitis.

PHYSICAL THERAPY FOR PATIENTS UNDERGOING THORACIC SURGERY

Currently, increasing numbers of patients are being referred for physical therapy before and after chest surgery, either for various forms of exercise, the use of some modality to relieve pain, or for postural or breathing exercises to help correct deformities resulting from the surgery.

The patient who has had surgery for lung abscess or cyst, empyema, bronchiectasis, or chronic hemothorax will, in most cases, develop marked changes in body posture unless preventive measures are taken: the cervical curve of his spine will be exaggerated, his head will tilt toward the unoperated side, and his shoulders will tilt downward and forward causing the chest to appear flattened. The lateral curvature of his spine will also be exaggerated (scoliosis), causing him to carry the hip on the affected side higher than the one on the nonaffected side. Therefore, the objectives in physical therapy for these patients are not only to relieve pain and improve pulmonary function but also to prevent or correct postural deformitie through the use of modalities that will strengthen the muscle involved, restore or maintain range of motion in joints, and thus help to prevent the patient from becoming a "ches cripple."

Therapeutic exercises and postural drainage are of greates importance in the accomplishment of these physical therapy objectives. Other modalities, such as ultraviolet therapy and heat supplied by infrared radiation, hot wet packs, bakers, or diathermy, may be of benefit in conjunction with the exercise program; however, these modalities are also sometimes prescribed for reducing pain, relaxing muscles, and improving circulation in the chest wall.

Preoperative Physical Therapy

Whenever possible, the patient should be seen by the physica therapist for several days preceding surgery. He should be taught diaphragmatic breathing technique, how to cough effectively, proper bed posture, the procedure for postura drainage, and shoulder, arm, and leg exercises. He should have time to practice these exercises under supervision so that he will know how to carry them out postoperatively. He needs also to understand why it is important to perform these exercises and procedures faithfully both before and after surgery.

Postoperative Procedures and Exercises

Postoperatively, the physical therapist is concerned primarily with helping the patient to maintain proper bed posture, to practice diaphragmatic breathing, and to maintain range of motion of the shoulder and scapula.

The immediate postoperative phase encompasses the first two postoperative days. Breathing exercises are started early and mobilization of the involved side, using selected procedures, may be encouraged. Physical therapy activities should be planned so as not to interfere with any drainage tubes or dressings. As the patient progresses, the exercises are adapted so they may be performed in the sitting position and finally in the standing position.

While still in bed, the patient should be helped to maintain good body posture. To help keep the body in proper alignment, a small pillow may be placed under his head and another one under the unoperated side. The therapist should support the patient during coughing and diaphragmatic breathing exercises.

While in the supine position, the patient can also be taught to flex the arm on the affected side, an important exercise for maintaining mobility and the functional use of the shoulder girdle, and for preventing deformity.

The patient may be out of bed on the second postoperative day and active physical therapy should be begun within 48 hours of the surgery. Exercises for maintaining proper posture when sitting, standing, and walking are emphasized. The various exercises are performed progressively according to the patient's physical condition.

Diaphragmatic breathing exercises should be practiced regularly. The patient holds the muscles of the chest and ribs tight while the therapist places one hand lightly on the chest, to see that it does not move, and the other hand on the patient's abdomen. The patient inhales while starting low down to balloon the abdominal wall up against the therapist's hand as far as he can; he then exhales, still not permitting the chest muscles to move.

The therapist should also assist the patient in the performance of various chest-expansion exercises. This usually involves placing one hand over the area to be exercised and having the patient inhale against the pressure of the therapist's hand. Any well-trained, experienced physical therapist will know how to demonstrate and give any type of chest-expansion exercises the physician may order for a particular patient.

Active assistive shoulder exercises and full active movement of the shoulder should be started early, including flexion, abduction, external rotation, horizontal adduction, and internal rotation.

To strengthen the upper abdominal muscles used in breathing, the patient should be in the supine position and raise his head, shoulders, and trunk as far as he can without coming to a sitting position. To strengthen the lower abdominals, the patient, again in the supine position, rolls his pelvis backward until it is flat on the surface of the bed and pulls upward and inward with his lower abdominal muscles. Then, with his knees flexed and with his pelvis and his feet flat on the bed, he straightens first one leg and then the other by sliding the heel along the surface of the bed.

To exercise the oblique abdominals the patient lies supinely on the bed, rolls his trunk to a sitting position, and twists to the right while reaching with the left hand toward the right knee; then he repeats the exercise while twisting his trunk to the left and reaching toward the left knee.

Physical Therapy for Lobectomy Patients

Lobectomy, the removal of part or all of one or more lobes of one or both lungs, is most commonly performed for bronchiectasis. It is especially suitable for the young patient in whom only one lobe is affected. However, if two lobes are affected and the remaining tissue is healthy, both lobes may be removed.

Certain complications attend lobectomies, the most important from the physical therapist's standpoint being the collapse of the remaining lobes. Collapse may occur as a result of obstruction in one or more bronchi by mucus or pus.

The immediate objective of physical therapy for the patient who has had a lobectomy is to prevent the accumulation of secretions while maintaining full expansion of the remaining lobes. To accomplish this the physical therapist assists the patient to perform breathing exercises, to carry out the postural drainage procedure, and to cough effectively. The breathing exercises are especially important; the patient should be encouraged to put particular stress on exhalation while carrying out the exercises. Diaphragmatic breathing exercises should be performed at least twice daily for the first few days.

Physical Therapy for Patients Who Have Had Thorcoplasty

Thorcoplasty is a surgical procedure involving the partial or total resection of any number of ribs to produce collapse of the chest wall, to obliterate the pleural cavity, or to reduce the thoracic space. Various muscles are affected by the surgery, including the trapezius, latissimus dorsi, serratus anterior, rhomboids, pectoralis, and scalenus; their origins and insertions may also be altered to varying degrees.

When the restraining action of the symmetrically opposite muscles is removed, the muscles on the unoperated side begin to shorten. On the operated side the shoulder rises, causing the scapula to "wing," the abdominal muscles to relax, the hip on the unoperated side to rise and thus tilt upward, and the head to tilt toward the shoulder of the unoperated side. To minimize these effects, infrared radiation is often applied for about 20 minutes to relieve pain, and is followed by breathing exercises. Fatigue should be avoided.

The patient should be taught diaphragmatic breathing and shoulder exercises, particularly rotation, flexion, and adduction, and scapular adduction. He is taught proper bed posture and positioning, encouraged to use the arm on his operated side to prevent atrophy and contracture, and cautioned to avoid fatigue.

IV

PHYSICAL THERAPY FOR GERIATRIC PATIENTS

The physician in general practice often has many patients in the older age group. Since chronic, degenerative diseases constitute the major medical problems of geriatric patients, the physician will find that, in addition to whatever medical treatment he has in mind, certain physical therapy modalities will often be helpful in restoring, at least partially, certain lost functions.

Several physiological changes that affect older people's response to treatment should be kept in mind when physical therapy modalities that are prescribed do not produce the expected results:

Gradual desiccation of tissues: Frequently, tissue changes in older people cause the skin to become thin, dry, and wrinkled — a condition that may influence results from the use of application of heat.

Gradual slowing down in the process of tissue repair: This change results from gradual retardation of cell division and capacity for cell growth. Because of this factor, moderation in intensity and prolongation in time of some physical therapy applications may be required to obtain satisfactory results.

Gradual retardation in the rate of tissue oxidation: This change requires the patient to avoid intense heat or vigorous exercise.

Decreased speed, strength, and endurance of skeletoneuromuscular reactions: Because of this change, it is important for the physical therapist and physician to make certain that muscle reeducation and all types of exercise be given in moderation, less frequently, and for shorter periods of time than are prescribed for younger people.

Progressive degeneration and atrophy of nervous system tissues: Changes in the nervous system are often the cause of impaired vision, hearing, memory, attention span, and mental application in elderly persons.

Pathologic conditions most commonly seen in the aged include: (1) cardiovascular disorders — arteriosclerosis, hypertension, and coronary artery disease; (2) arthritis and related disorders of the musculoskeletal system; (3) metabolic disorders, including diabetes and gout; and (4) cancer. It must be remembered also that disorders and conditions following trauma to the nervous system are frequent therapeutic problems of the aged, and that these people are subject to the same acute diseases that attack younger people.

Bruises, contusions, strain, sprains, fracture, dislocation, and the very common low back syndrome are all conditions that may be seen in the elderly, as well as myositis, tenosynovitis, bursitis, and osteoporosis. (These conditions are described elsewhere in this book. See index.) The neurologic conditions seen in the elderly are frequently associated with vascular degeneration of cerebral blood vessels. Such conditions include hemiplegia, sciatica, paralysis agitans, multiple sclerosis, and Parkinson's disease.

CARDIOVASCULAR DISORDERS

Inadequate treatment of acute cardiac conditions promotes the development of thrombi in the veins of the lower extremities. Early passive movement two or three times a day is considered of value in preventing this complication. When the patient has regained some strength, the physical therapist instructs him in active exercises that can be performed in bed. The exercises must be individualized for each patient.

ARTHRITIS AND RELATED DISORDERS

A very common complaint in older patients is pain and stiffness of one or more joints, which is frequently caused by arthritis. All types of arthritis may be found in older people, but osteoarthritis is by far the most common.

Osteoarthritis affects mainly the large weight-bearing joints. It develops from a nutritional inadequacy, such as the loss of calcium, which affects bones and articulating surfaces. It is also frequently associated with repeated minor trauma and obesity. Crepitus is frequently noted in the larger joints of the extremities. The use of physical therapy modalities in the treatment of osteoarthritis is part of the general therapeutic plan. Heat is applied in various forms, such as infrared rays, diathermy, hot packs, and baking. Massage and active exercise for specific joints are also prescribed. Other aspects of treatment include weight reduction (very important), proper medication, and corrective orthopedic measuers.

The details of treatment for osteoarthritis are adjusted to the individual's specific needs, but the proper use of heat, massage, and regulated exercise are of greatest benefit to these patients.

Rheumatoid arthritis is treated primarily with drug therapy, but physical therapy modalities, used in conjunction with the drugs, play an important part in the treatment.

GOUT

Gout is encountered in elderly patients but, usually, it has been diagnosed and controlled with medical treatment at an earlier age. Treatment consists of drug therapy in conjunction with the use of various physical therapy modalities.

Appendix I
SAMPLE FORMS

Appendix IA. Sample Form for Ordering Treatment

REQUEST FOR PHYSICAL THERAPY TREATMENT

Outpatient _____
Inpatient (room no. _____)
Admission no. _____
Date _____

Name _____ Age _____

Address _____ Tel. No. _____

Diagnoses _____
          primary (must have)   secondary

Parts to be treated _____

Instructions _____
              (frequency, duration, dosage, etc.)

Check (✓) below treatment desired

____ Baker

____ Cervical traction
    ____ intermittent
    ____ continuous

____ Diathermy

____ Electrical stimulation
    ____ galvanic
    ____ faradic

____ Exercise
    ____ active   ____ resistive
    ____ passive   ____ muscle
                     training
    ____ assistive ____ postural
                      exercises

____ Hubbard tub

____ Infrared

____ Iontophoresis

____ Jobst unit

____ Hot packs

____ Massage
    ____ sedative
    ____ stimulating

____ Paraffin bath

____ Sauna bath

____ Sitz bath

____ Ultrasound

____ Ultraviolet
    ____ local
    ____ general

____ Whirlpool bath
    ____ general
    ____ arm
    ____ leg

Special information for the therapist (whether patient has a cardiac condition, diabetes, etc.) _____

_____

Return to physician for checkup _____

Physician's signature _____

RECORD OF PHYSICAL THERAPY TREATMENTS

Inpatient (room)_____ Outpatient_____
Week of _____

Name _____ Age _____ Admission no._____

Address_____

Diagnosis (must have)_____ Parts treated _____

Frequency of treatment (indicate daily, 2 or 3 times weekly, etc.)_____

_____

Check below treatment administered.

Special instructions to the therapist_____

_____

_____

Doctor	Mon	Tues	Wed	Thurs	Fri	Sat	Sun
Baker							
Cervical traction - intermittent							
Cervical traction - continuous							
Diathermy							
Electrical stimulation - galvanic							
Electrical stimulation - faradic							
Exercise - active							
Exercise - passive							
Exercise - assistive							
Exercise - resistive							
Exercise - muscle training							
Exercise - postural							
Hubbard tub							
Infrared							
Iontophoresis							
Jobst unit							
Hot packs							
Massage - sedative							
Massage - stimulating							
Paraffin bath							
Sauna bath							
Sitz bath							
Ultrasound							
Ultraviolet - local							
Ultraviolet - general							
Whirlpool bath - general							
Whirlpool bath - arm							
Whirlpool bath - leg							

Appendix II

EQUIPMENT AND APPARATUS USED FOR GIVING PHYSICAL THERAPY

Bakers
Bicycle (stationary)
Canes
Cervical traction unit
Crutches
Diathermy machine
Electrical machine capable of producing galvanic, faradic, and sinusoidal current
Exercise mat
Exercise pulleys
Exercise table
Full-length mirror
Goniometer (for measuring motion or flexion in various joints)
Hand exercise equipment
Hubbard tank
Hydrocollator (cold pack and hot pack)
Infrared lamps
Jobst unit (for promoting venous and lymphatic return)
Medcollator

Overhead sling
Paraffin bath (tub or pan)
Parallel bars
Pulley weights
Sauna bath
Sayre spinal traction apparatus (head sling)
Scale (for weighing patients)
Shoulder wheel
Stairs
Stretcher
Supinator
Pronator
Tilt table
Treatment table
Ultrasonic machine
Ultraviolet lamps
Walkers (all types)
Weights (of different denominations and types, for measuring resistive activity)
Wheelchair
Whirlpool bath tubs (several sizes)

Appendix III
MODALITIES RECOMMENDED FOR COMMONLY DIAGNOSED CONDITIONS AND CONDITIONS IN WHICH THEY ARE CONTRAINDICATED

MODALITY	INDICATED IN	CONTRAINDICATED IN
Breathing exercise	asthma; atelectasis; emphysema	
Buerger's exercise	Buerger's disease	
Codman's exercise	bursitis	
Contrast bath	arteriosclerosis obliterans	
Diaphragmatic breathing	abdominal atony; asthma; bronchitis; constipation; dislocations; emphysema; herniated disk; neuritis; peripheral vascular disease (low intensity); pleurisy; prolonged bed rest	
Diathermy	abscess; arthritis; bronchitis; bursitis; coccygodynia; colitis; contusions; dislocations; epicondylitis; fibrositis; fractures; hematoma; laryngitis; low back pain; lumbago; muscle spasm; myalgia; myositis; nephritis; neuralgia; pelvic inflammatory disease; pleurisy; pneumonia; prostatitis; pyelonephritis; salpingitis; sciatica; sinusitis; sprains; strains; synovitis; tenosynovitis; torticollis	acute arthritis; acute cellulitis; acute inflammatory processes; menstruation; peripheral nerve injuries over areas in which appreciation of heat has been lost or impaired; pregnancy (if treatment of abdomen, pelvis, or lower back is required); suspected malignant growth; tendency to hemorrhage
Electric stimulation	Bell's palsy; facial paralysis; hemiplegia	
Ethyl chloride aerosol	sprains; strains	

Reprinted from Tice's *Practice of Medicine* (1969), vol. 1, chap. 20, by permission of the Medical Department, Harper & Row, Publishers, Inc., Hagerstown, Maryland.

MODALITY	INDICATED IN	CONTRAINDICATED IN
Exercise	adhesions; amputations; arteriosclerosis obliterans; atrophy; Bell's palsy; brachialgia; causalgia; contractures; contusions; dislocations; epicondylitis; fibrositis; fractures; hemiplegia; intervertebral disk lesion; kyphosis; lordosis; low back pain; lumbago; myalgia; myositis; paralysis; peripheral nerve lesion; peripheral vascular disease; scars; sciatica; scoliosis; spondylolisthesis; sprains; strains; synovitis	
Hot packs or compresses	abscess; adhesions; arthritis; Bell's palsy; contractures; contusions; dislocations; epicondylitis; fibrositis; fractures; frozen joints; hematoma; low back pain; muscle spasm; myalgia; myositis; neuralgia; neuritis; pleurisy; radiculitis; scars, sinusitis; spasm; sprains; strains; synovitis; torticollis	
Hubbard tank	arthritis; burns; fractures; low back pain; neuritis	
Ice packs	Bell's palsy; contusions; sprains; strains	
Infrared radiation	abscess; arthritis; Bell's palsy; bronchitis; bursitis; carbuncles; coccygodynia; contusions; decubitus; dislocations; epicondylitis; facial paralysis; fibrositis; fractures; frozen joints; furuncles; hematoma, intercostal neuralgia; laryngitis; low back pain; lumbago; lymphangitis; mumps; muscle spasm; myalgia; myositis; neuritis; peripheral vascular disease phlebitis; pleurisy; pleurodynia; radiculitis; sinusitis; sprains; strains; synovitis; tenosynovitis; thrombophlebitis; torticollis	anesthetic areas; areas under which metal or plastic devices are emplaced; cardiovascular disease; hyperpyrexia; malignant tumors; peripheral vascular disease (intense local application); sensory disturbances leading to loss of perception of heat or cold or both

MODALITY	INDICATED IN	CONTRAINDICATED IN
Ion transfer	arteriosclerosis obliterans; peripheral vascular disease; Raynaud's disease	
Tobst unit	peripheral vascular disease; Raynaud's disease	
Massage	adhesions; amputations; arthritis; atrophy; Bell's palsy; bursitis; contusions; dislocations; facial paralysis; fibrositis; fractures; hematoma; hemiplegia; low back pain; lumbago; muscle spasm; myalgia; neuralgia; peripheral nerve lesion; scars; sprains; strains; torticollis	acute burns; dermatitis; acutely inflamed joints; advanced arteriosclerosis; nephritis; increased pain, swelling, or stiffness in joint following massage; infectious diseases; phlebitis; lymphangitis; presence of intra-abdominal organic disease; suspected local malignancy
Moist heat	amputations; anal tissue; carbuncles; furuncles; hemorrhoids; tenosynovitis; wounds	
Muscle stimulation	atrophy; hemiplegia; paralysis; peripheral nerve lesion	
Neuromuscular reeducation	cerebrovascular accident; cerebral palsy; Guillain-Barré syndrome; multiple sclerosis; Parkinson's disease; poliomyelitis	
Paraffin bath	arthritis; brachialgia; contusions; gout; epicondylitis; fibrositis; fractures; myalgia; myositis; scars; sprains; strains; synovitis; tenosynovitis	dermatologic disorders; skin broken or damaged; use with caution when patient's ability to tolerate heat is impaired
Postural training	low back pain	
Sitz bath	cystitis; prostatitis	
Sodium salicylate iontophoresis	sciatica	
Stretching exercise	burns	
Traction	arthritis; brachialgia; causalgia; cervical syndrome; intervertebral disk lesion; neuralgia; neuritis; radiculitis; sciatica; sprain; strain; whiplash injury	

MODALITY	INDICATED IN	CONTRAINDICATED IN
Ultrasound	adhesions; arthritis; bursitis; coccygodynia; contractures; contusions; dislocations; epicondylitis; fibrositis; fractures; herpes zoster; intercostal neuralgia; low back pain; muscle spasm; myalgia; myositis; nephritis; neuroma; nocturnal paresthesia; peripheral vascular disease; plantar wart; sciatica; spondylitis; sprains; synovitis; tenosynovitis; torticollis; whiplash injury	acute infectious paralysis; caution when treating peripheral vascular disease; do not apply to plexus, brain, spinal cord, eyes, ears, heart reproductive organs, metaphysis of growing bone; sensory paralysis
Ultraviolet	acne; alopecia areata; asthma; boils; decubitus ulcer; eczema; furuncles; herpes zoster; impetigo; lupus vulgaris; psoriasis; tuberculosis; wounds	advanced arteriosclerosis; heart disease; hyperthyroidism, diabetes; dermatitis; pulmonary tuberculosis; renal or hepatic insufficiency
Whirlpool bath	adhesions; arthritis; burns; fractures; frozen joints; low back pain; peripheral nerve lesion; peripheral vascular disease; scars; sprains; strains; synovitis; tenosynovitis; varicose ulcers; wounds	

Appendix IV
MODALITIES USED
IN PHYSICAL THERAPY

AGENT OR MODALITY	PURPOSE OR EFFECT	METHOD OR MEANS OF APPLICATION
Cold (cryotherapy)	Analgesic Decrease in metabolic rate Reduction of spasticity Vasoconstriction followed by vasodilatation	Cold whirlpool Ethyl chloride aerosol Ice packs
Electricity (electrotherapy)	Chronaxy Common ion transfer (iontophoresis) for sedation or stimulation Electrodiagnosis Electromyography (high voltage generators) Muscle stimulation Retardation of atrophy Strength duration curve	Low voltage generators (faradic and galvanic)
Exercise	Combat atrophy of disuse and debilitation General conditioning Maintain or increase range of motion, muscle strength, endurance, coordination, and balance	Active Assistive Passive Progressive resistive Resistive Bakers
Heat (thermotherapy)	Analgesic Increase in metabolic rate Sedation Vasodilatation	Electric heating pad Hubbard tank Hydrocollator pads Infrared lamp Microtherm Moist air cabinet Paraffin bath Short wave diathermy Ultrasound Whirlpool bath

AGENT OR MODALITY	PURPOSE OR EFFECT	METHOD OR MEANS OF APPLICATION
Manipulation	Increase range of motion Prevent or reduce contracture, subluxations Stretching	Manual or weights
Massage	Increase circulation Loosen scar tissue Reduce edema Sedation or stimulation	Friction Kneading Percussion Stroking
Rays (actinotherapy)	Bactericidal Increase in metabolic rate Pigmentation	Ultraviolet rays
Traction	Relieve pressure	Manual or machine, Sayre sling
Water (hydrotherapy)	Cleansing Reduction of edema Reduction of spasticity Relaxation Sedation	Whirlpool bath Hubbard tank

Appendix V
MUSCLES THAT TAKE PART
IN VARIOUS BODY MOVEMENTS

PART MOVED	MOVEMENT	MUSCLES*
Head and neck	Flexion (bending neck forward)	Sternocleidomastoid
	Extension (bending neck backward)	Trapezius; Sacrospinalis
Trunk	Flexion (bending trunk forward)	Rectus abdominis
	Extension (bending upper part of trunk backward)	Sacrospinalis, Iliocostalis lumborum
	Rotation (bending trunk side to side)	Obliquus externus, Obliquus internus
Hip	Flexion (bending hip forward)	Iliopsoas
	Extension (bending hip backward)	Gluteus maximus
	Adduction	Adductor magnus, Adductor longus, Adductor brevis
	External rotation	Obturator iternus, Obturator externus, Quadratus femoris, Piriformis
	Internal rotation	Gluteus minimus, Tensor fascia lata
Knee	Flexion (bending knee)	Biceps femoris, Senitendinosis, Semimembranosus
	Extension (extending leg forward)	Quadriceps group (Rectus femoris, Vastus lateralis, Vastus medius, Vastus intermedius)
Ankle	Plantar flexion	Gastrocnemius, Soleus
	Dorsiflexion with inversion (turning foot forward and inward)	Tibialis anterior
	Plantar flexion with inversion (turning foot downward and inward)	Tibialis posterior
	Plantar flexion with eversion (turning foot outward and downward)	Peroneus brevis, Peroneus longus

*This list includes only the major muscles involved in movements. It is intended as a guide to the health worker in prescribing physical therapy treatments.

PART MOVED	MOVEMENT	MUSCLES
Toes	Flexion	Flexor digitorum longus, Flexor digitorum brevis, Lumbricales
	Extension	Extensor digitorum longus, Extensor digitorum brevis
	Flexion of great toe	Flexor hallucis longus, Flexor hallucis brevis
	Extension of great toe	Extensor hallucis longus, Extensor hallucis brevis
Scapula	Adduction	Trapezius (middle part), Rhomboideus
	Abduction	Serratus anterior
	Elevation	Trapezius (upper part)
	Backward depression	Trapezius (lower part)
Shoulder	Flexion	Deltoideus anterior
	Extension	Latissimus dorsi, Teres major
	Horizontal adduction	Pectoralis major
	Horizontal abduction	Deltoideus posterior
	Internal rotation	Subscapularis
	External rotation	Teres minor, Infraspinatus
Elbow	Flexion	Biceps brachii, Brachioradialis
	Extension	Triceps
	Supination of forearm	Biceps brachii, Supinator
	Pronation of forearm	Pronator teres, Pronator quadratus
Wrist	Flexion	Flexor carpi radialis, Flexor carpi ulnaris
	Extension	Extensor carpi radialis longus, Extensor carpi radialis brevis, Extensor carpi ulnaris
Fingers	Flexion	Lumbricales, Flexor digitorum sublimus, Flexor digitorum profundus
	Extension	Extensor digitorum communis
	Adduction	Interossei palmares
	Abduction	Interossei dorsalis, Abductor digiti quinti (little finger)
	Opposition (little finger)	Opponens digiti quinti

PART MOVED	MOVEMENT	MUSCLES
Thumb	Flexion	Flexor pollicis brevis, Flexor pollicis longus
	Extension	Extensor pollicis longus, Extensor pollicis brevis
	Adduction	Adductor obliquus pollicis, Adductor transversus pollicis
	Abduction	Abductor pollicis longus, Abductor pollicis brevis
	Opposition	Opponens pollicis

READINGS IN PHYSICAL THERAPY

American Lung Association. *What You Can Do about Your Breathing*. New York: The Association, 1975.

Brunnstrom, S. *Movement Therapy in Hemiplegia*. New York: Harper & Row, 1970.

Bryan, C.D., and Taylor, J.P. *Manual of Respiratory Therapy*. St. Louis: C.V. Mosby, 1973.

Burak, J. *There Goes My Aching Back*. Birmingham, Ala.: Banner, 1975.

Cailliet, R. *Neck and Arm Pain*. Philadelphia: F.A. Davis, 1964.

_____. *Shoulder Pain*. Philadelphia: F.A. Davis, 1966.

_____. *Foot and Ankle Pain*. Philadelphia: F.A. Davis, 1968.

_____. *Low Back Pain Syndrome*, 2d ed. Philadelphia: F.A. Davis, 1968.

_____. *Knee Pain and Disability*. Philadelphia: F.A. Davis, 1973.

_____. *Hand Pain and Impairment*. Philadelphia: F.A. Davis, 1975.

_____. *Scoliosis*. Philadelphia: F.A. Davis, 1975.

Cash, J.E. (ed.) *Chest, Heart, and Vascular Disorders for Physiotherapists*. Philadelphia: J.B. Lippincott, 1975

Covalt, N.K. *Bed Exercises for Convalescent Patients*. Springfield, Ill.: Charles C Thomas, 1968.

Department of Health, Education, and Welfare. *Strike Back at Stroke*. Washington, D.C.: U.S. Government Printing Office, 1961.

Downer, A.H. *Physical Therapy Procedures: Selected Techniques*. Springfield, Ill.: Charles C. Thomas, 1974.

Hollander, J.L., and McCarty, D.J., Jr. *Arthritis and Allied Conditions*, 8th ed. Philadelphia: Lea and Febiger, 1972.

Huddleston, O.L. *Therapeutic Exercises: Kinesiotherapy*. Philadelphia: F.A. Davis, 1961.

Jokl, E. *The Scope of Exercise in Rehabilitation*. Springfield, Ill.: Charles C. Thomas, 1964.

_____. *Physiology of Exercise*. Springfield, Ill.: Charles C. Thomas, 1971.

Kraus, H. *Backache, Stress and Tension*. New York: Simon and Schuster, 1969.

———. *Clinical Treatment of Back and Neck Pain*. New York: McGraw-Hill Book Co., 1970.

Krusen, F.H. *Handbook of Physical Medicine and Rehabilitation*, 2d ed. Philadelphia: W.B. Saunders Co., 1971.

Pedro, C. *Finger Acupressure*. Los Angeles: Price, Stern and Sloan, 1974.

Rusk, H.A. *Rehabilitation Medicine*, 3d ed. St. Louis: C.V. Mosby Co., 1971.

Shriber, W.J. *A Manual of Electrotherapy*, 4th ed. Philadelphia: Lea & Febiger, 1975.

Tappan, F.M. *Massage Techniques*. New York: Macmillan, 1961.

Winter, R. *A Pain in the Neck*. New York: Grosset and Dunlap, 1974.

INDEX

DUE